South-Western

EXPLORING DESKTOP PUBLISHING

A PROJECTS APPROACH

Scott D. Korb
Normandy High School
Parma, Ohio

Reviewers:

Rose Corgan
Raymond Walters College
Cincinnati, Ohio

Priscilla Kotyk
Acton Boxborough Regional School District
Acton, Massachusetts

JOIN US ON THE INTERNET
WWW: http://www.thomson.com
EMAIL: findit@kiosk.thomson.com   A service of I(T)P®

South-Western Educational Publishing
an International Thomson Publishing company I(T)P®

Cincinnati • Albany, NY • Belmont, CA • Bonn • Boston • Detroit • Johannesburg • London • Madrid
Melbourne • Mexico City • New York • Paris • Singapore • Tokyo • Toronto • Washington

ISBN 0-538-71803-X
Printed in the United States of America

I(T)P*

International Thomson Publishing

South-Western Educational Publishing is a division of International Thomson
Publishing, Inc. The ITP trademark is used under license.

Managing Editor	Janie F. Schwark
Project Manager	Dave Lafferty
Marketing Manager	Kent Christensen
Design Coordinator	Ann Small
Development and Production	Thompson Steele Production Services

CONTENTS

PREFACE

This text is an introduction to desktop publishing for use in high school, college, or continuing education courses. It includes 40 generic lab projects, which work with any desktop publishing software; the projects take approximately 110 hours to complete. They range in scope from simple reports and newsletters to complex advertisements, flyers, and business reports. The first projects are much less complex than those at the end of the text. The projects and directions for completion of the projects assume that students have basic computer skills.

Instructors may use these materials for a semester course in desktop publishing assuming that they assign every project. The text can also serve as a component of a semester-long computer applications course. (This approach would probably require the instructor to skip the last unit, which contains some rather lengthy projects.)

Along with the projects, the text includes an appendix introducing students to the principles of good design. Such principles are essential elements for students who are learning about desktop publishing.

The Teacher's Manual that accompanies this text includes teaching tips/suggestions for each project, lesson plans, handouts, quizzes, tests, a final examination, and a printout of the project and test solutions. Some of the project and test solutions that are printed in the manual are not to scale. The art that we used in creating some of the projects may not be available in the desktop publishing programs that your students are using. Feel free to substitute other art. We have included project templates (in a simple text format) for Projects 1, 2, 7–20, 22, 23, 25–30, 32, 35, 36, and 37 on disks for both the PC and Macintosh. These disks also contain art that students can use for Projects 13, 14, 16, 17, 19–22, 26, 28, 30, 32.

In addition, there are also disks for both the PC (Microsoft Publisher 2.0, Microsoft Publisher 3.0, and PageMaker 6.0) and Macintosh (PageMaker 6.0) that include the project solutions.

UNIT ONE
Introduction to Typing Text and Drawing

Objectives

After completing this unit you will be able to:

- Create text frames (text blocks).

- Change fonts and use bold.

- Center text inside text frames (text blocks) and center text frames (text blocks) horizontally between margin guides.

- Spell check.

- Save to disk and print.

- Center text (vertically) inside text frames (text blocks)

- Use numbered and bulleted lists and two-column text frames or adjacent text frames (text blocks).

- Change margin guides.

- Draw lines, boxes, circles, arrows, and predrawn shapes.

- Move and resize drawn objects and copy and paste objects.

- Use grid or snap-to feature.

- Use zoom (magnify).

- Group objects and use shading to fill objects.

- Center objects in relationship with other objects.

- Create a pie chart.

- Layer objects.

- Type inside of a predrawn shape.

Directions

For all projects	For this project
1. Set font to Times New Roman. (Note: Some projects will use more than one font.) 2. You decide what margins to use. 3. Position and size frames and other objects approximately as shown. 4. For all borders use approximate thickness shown. 5. Projects shown may not always be to scale visually. 6. Always check spelling, save to disk, and print to paper.	1. Use size 10 for name line. Use size 16 bold for the main title; center it. Use size 14 bold for the four subheads. Use size 12 for the text. 2. Create separate text frame (block) for each title and paragraph. For the main title, leave some extra space on the left and right. Resize frames to eliminate extra space either vertically or horizontally for the subhead. 3. Use P1 for file name.

Your Name   Project 1

FEATURES OF DESKTOP PUBLISHING

Manipulation of Objects

Anything you create in a desktop publisher is an **object**. Objects include text frames, pictures such as clip art, tables, drawn objects like lines and boxes, and objects pasted from other software such as spreadsheets or charts. A chief advantage of desktop publishing is the ability to easily manipulate an object. This includes the ability to move an object to any position on the page, resize the object, and copy and paste the object.

Typing in Columns

You can place text (typed materials) into columns. You can easily change the number of and the width of the columns. You can also control how the information flows from one column to another or arrange text to flow to another column on the same page or to a column on another page.

Drawing Tools

Depending on the software, various drawing tools are usually offered. These typically allow the user to draw lines, boxes, circles, and other shapes. Boxes, circles, and other enclosed shapes can be filled with patterns and colors. You can place drawn objects anywhere on the page.

Special Word Effects

Special word effects usually include the ability to change how words look, for example, changing font and size or changing the shape and angle of words. You may be able to stretch letters out within a word or stretch words on a line. Rotation commands may allow you to change the angle of an entire frame of words so the words print up and down on the page.

Directions

Frames: Create frames as shown. You may increase the spacing around the frames to avoid crowding. **Font sizes for heads:** 10 for name line and heads in first two boxes; 28 bold for "PTA NEWS"; 12 for "A Monthly ..."; 14 bold for "From the president ...," "HIGH SCHOOL ...," and "News Bits"; 20 bold for "CAR WASH."	**Font sizes for text:** 9, 10, 12, and 14 in various frames. Use bullets and two-column frames as shown below. Use centering as shown. Use P2 for file name.

Your Name   Project 2

Published by the Tri-City PTA Council	# PTA NEWS	Volume 6 October 10, 1998

A Monthly Newsletter for Parents of the Happy Valley School District

From the president of the PTA:

This is going to be a very exciting school year. I am sure that you will want to attend many of the sporting events. The high school football and volleyball teams, which are undefeated this season, value your continued support. The junior high science fair will be held on November 5. Students from 7th and 8th grade will exhibit science projects they completed recently. If you have not joined the PTA yet this year, please do so soon. Have a great year.

HIGH SCHOOL THIS MONTH

- Two football games
- Three volleyball games
- Fall dance
- PTA membership drive
- Band concert
- Booster club candy sale
- Drama Club tryouts
- Financial aid meeting
- Driver's education signup
- Language club meeting

CAR WASH

SATURDAYS

High School

9am-2pm

This newsletter was printed on recycled paper and fully paid for by donations to the PTA.

News Bits

Scholarships. Last year, students received over $2 million in scholarships and financial aid. This included over $50,000 in PTA funds, awarded to graduating seniors.

Dropout Rate. Our district has one of the lowest dropout rates in the country as nationally recognized by *USA Today*.

Belt-Tightening. Overall spending levels for the school district are less than last year as a result of cutbacks in administrative positions, transportation, reduced insurance premiums for health care, and savings in energy and maintenance.

Awards. The June issue of *American Magazine* rated the district as an A for academic performance. Last year, the State Department of Education ranked the junior high computer program in the top ten for developing innovative courses.

Directions

Getting started
1. Use the desktop publishing (dtp) drawing tools to draw the graphics.
2. If available, use snap-to-ruler marks or grid command.

Main title: Use size 26. Center over the chart later.

Outer bars (not the insides of the bars)
1. Draw one bar (just the outline—nothing inside). →
2. Copy and paste three more bars.
3. The bars must be the same width.
4. Drag bars to evenly space apart. Line up on the bottom edge.
5. Resize the bars vertically to approximate the correct heights.

Inside bars
1. Divide bars into sections by drawing boxes on top of the current bars.
2. Add shading (fill) patterns (if possible on your software). Pick any patterns desired, but each vertical section must have the same pattern.

Numbers on left: Space evenly apart and line up on left edge.

Years: Type each year in a separate frame. Drag to center each year under each bar. Line up years on bottom edge.

Lines: Use thick line on left and bottom.

Legend
1. Draw one inside box. Then copy and paste two more. The boxes must be the same size.
2. Use the same shading (fill) patterns as below.
3. Use separate text frames for the descriptive text and line up on the left edge.
4. Draw a thick outer box around the legend. Type and center "Legend" above the outer box as shown.

Your Name   Project 3

SOCIAL SPENDING COSTS

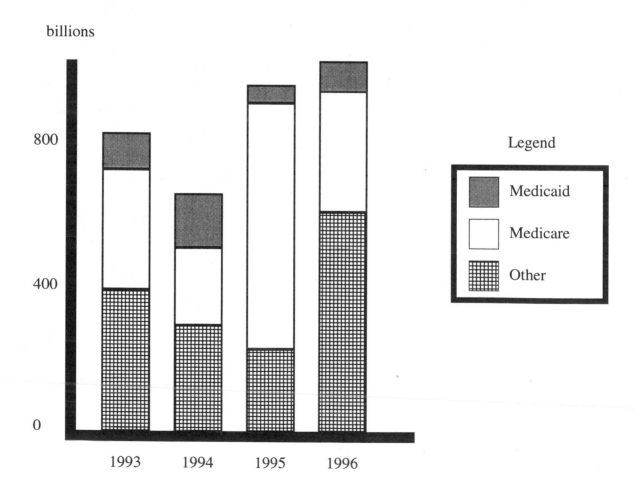

Directions

Getting started
1. Use the drawing tools to draw the graphics.
2. If available, use snap-to-ruler marks or grid.

Main title: Use smaller size font for second title. Center over the chart.

Drawing the first computer
1. Draw the top of the computer using the box tool.
2. Zoom in to do the rest of the computer.
3. After completing one computer, "group" the objects (if your software has this feature).
4. If needed, resize the computer.

Copy and paste the other computers: Computers must be placed equal distances apart both vertically and horizontally, and they must be lined up (left edge).

Graph creation
1. Draw thick lines on left and bottom.

2. Key numbers on left. Position equal distances apart and line up on left edge.
3. Key months and center under their respective bars. If your software has a line up objects command, see directions below. Otherwise, center them by dragging to position them.
4. Center the main titles over the chart.

Centering months using line up object command
1. When creating a text frame, estimate frame position and type a month.
2. Center the month inside the text frame.
3. Select the month (click it) and select the computer above it (do not group them).
4. Use the line up objects command to center horizontally (left to right).

Your Name   Project 4

SUPERNET COMPUTERS INC.

Sales (in thousands)

dollars

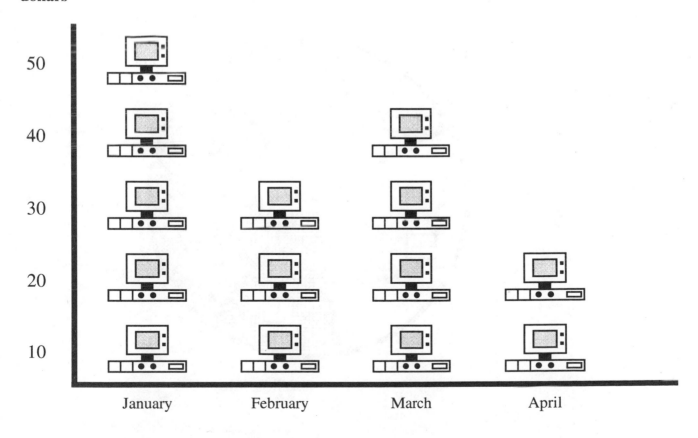

Directions

Getting started
1. Use the drawing tools to draw the graphics.
2. If available, use snap-to-ruler marks or grid.

Main title: Center title over the pie.

Pie and Slices (if your software has a pie symbol)
1. Use the pie symbol to draw one of the pie slices.
2. If needed, resize the symbol to establish the overall pie size.
3. Use the adjustment handles to resize and position the slice at the correct angle.
4. Copy and paste the slice.
5. Use the adjustment handles only (do not resize) to establish the second slice.
6. Drag the slice into position with the first slice.
7. Repeat the above steps to create other slices.
8. Group the entire pie chart.
9. Add shading to each slice.

Pie and Slices (if your software does not have a pie symbol)
1. Use the circle tool to draw the outer circle.
2. Type a period in the center of the circle.
3. Draw lines to create the slices.
4. Zoom in to make sure that lines attach properly. Note: With this method, you can't use shading.

Numbers inside the slices (all numbers frames must be the same size and all numbers must be the same font size)
1. Create a text frame outside of the pie. Include a border.
2. Type a number and center it in the frame.
3. Copy and paste it four times (for the other numbers).
4. Change the others to the correct numbers.
5. Move the numbers into the pie slices. Note: You may have to use the bring to front command or similar command to cause the numbered boxes to be on top of the pie slice.

Key the slice descriptions.

Your Name   Project 5

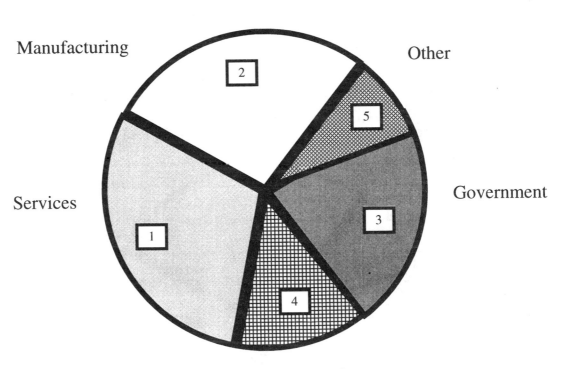

JOBS

Project 6 HOUSE AND FLOOR PLAN

Directions

Getting started
1. Use the drawing tools to draw the graphics.
2. If available, use snap-to-ruler marks or grid.

Draw the house
1. Use shading (fill patterns) if available on your software. Choose your own patterns.

2. The windows on the second floor must be the same size.
3. If available, use the following symbol for the garage:
4. For arrows, use lines with arrow option if available on your software.
5. Use black shading for windows on floor plan.

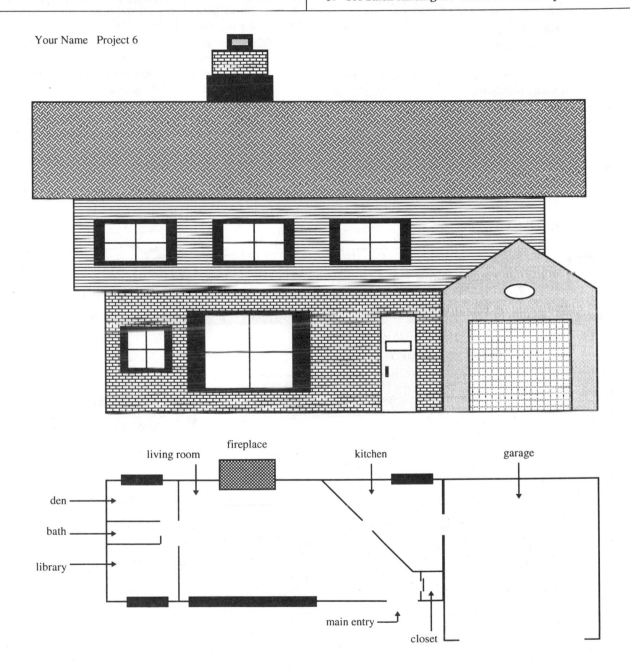

Your Name   Project 6

fireplace

living room

kitchen

garage

den

bath

library

main entry

closet

Directions

Title line

1. **Gas News** in bold, size approximately as shown; first letter of each word must be capitalized (this title is in one frame).
2. **Central Gas Co.** in bold, size 18; use predrawn symbol if available (stretch to fit words). Center the text frame left to right inside the symbol, then make the symbol and text frame one group.

Divider Line: Draw thick line.

Reading your gas meter

1. Set in bold, size 18.
2. If available, use Two-Column Frame, size 10 (or create two separate text frames).

Coupon tips

1. Size 14, bold.
2. Paragraph under title, size 10, use bullet, thick border line.
3. Center "Coupon Tips" within the frame and left to right with the text frame below it.

Meter circles

1. Draw the first one with everything inside (size 9 or 10 for numbers).
2. Group it and copy and paste three others.
3. Ungroup the last three. Then reposition the arrows and regroup each circle.
4. Space each circle evenly apart. Then group all four circles (one big group) and center left to right with the text frame above.

Titles under circles

1. Size 9 or 10.
2. Type on two lines and eliminate excess space.
3. Title frames must be the same height.
4. Center the words in their frames.
5. Ungroup the four circles (the big group only) and center each text frame left to right with the circle above it.

Words on right of circles: Use size 14.

Your Name   Project 7

Gas News

Central Gas Co.

Reading Your Gas Meter

Normally, our gas readers read and record the meter readings. However, occasionally you may be asked to verify the readings to make sure that you are not being overcharged.

Your meter has four dials. Each dial has a pointer that turns in opposite directions. When recording the numbers, use the smaller number when the pointer falls between two numbers. If the pointer falls between 8 and 0, read it as 8 because 0 is really 10.

When recording the numbers on your service card, be sure to record the numbers from left to right. The 4-digit number is in **cubic feet**.

Coupon Tips

⇒ Use double coupons when possible.
⇒ Circle the expiration dates so that you do not forget to use them.
⇒ Swap coupons with your friends.
⇒ Compare the savings with a generic product.

one million

one hundred thousand

ten thousand

one thousand

The meter reading for the meter shown on the left is 5378.

See directions on next two pages

Your Name   Project 8

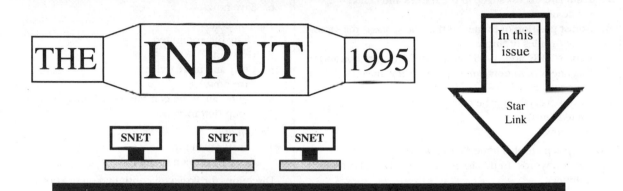

THE **INPUT** 1995

SNET   SNET   SNET

In this issue

Star Link

SNET Location

SNET is now located on the XYZ-TV Star Link network. With just a microcomputer, communications software, and a modem, you will be ready to access Star Link over regular telephone lines with **no on-line charges**.

SNET Membership

With one yearly membership fee, you will have unlimited access to this communications network 24 hours a day, 365 days a year. Whenever you want to use the Net, it will be ready.

STAR LINK Main Menu

Mail and tools

- Mail
- PBS on-line projects
- Einstein
- Student service
- Tools and utilities

Gateways

- Internet
- School news groups
- CNN newsroom
- Linkchat
- File library

Logging onto Star Link

You can use Star Link from home, the office, or school. All you need is a log-on code and a password. An application form is included on the back of this sheet. Fill it in and mail today.

Steps to log on

1. Turn on the modem.
2. Start your communications program.
3. Dial the Star Link number.
4. Type your log-on code.
5. Type your password.
6. When the menu appears, choose your desired item.

SNET Users

If you are outside of the calling area, you will be especially glad to know that Star Link has a statewide toll-free access number.

Star Link users will also have access to the Internet, libraries, databases, and other data sources through a collection of networks around the world. You can access other educational sites in this country and participate in forums, interest groups, and discussions.

NEXT

- * The WEB
- * New Resources
- * Security

ISSUE

TIP: Save often.

Border: Use thicker lines approximately as shown and draw top line between margin guides.

Main title (THE INPUT 1995)

1. Key the words; use bold and approximate font size shown. Use three text frames.
2. Eliminate excess space in the frames and center inside of frames.
3. Adjust position of frames so that the space is the same on both sides of "Input."
4. Center "THE" and "1995" with "INPUT" (top to bottom).
5. Use line tool to draw angled lines (they must connect—zoom in).
6. Group everything (the main title words and angled lines).
7. Save now.

Arrow group (In this issue, Star Link)

1. Key the words "In this issue". Use size 12 and center in frame.
2. Key the words "Star Link". Use a separate frame, size 10, center in frame.
3. Draw arrow (if available, use predrawn symbol). Size as needed. Note: if text frame blocks part of the arrow, use the send to back command on the text frame.
4. Center (left to right) each text frame with the arrow.
5. Group the arrow and text frames inside it.
6. Save now.

The computer

1. Draw the computer,
2. Group it.
3. Copy and paste twice.
4. Save now.
5. Center all of the computers (as one group) under title group (left to right).

Bottom line

1. Shorter than top line.
2. Center between layout guides.

Directions for Project 8 continued on next page.

Your Name   Project 8

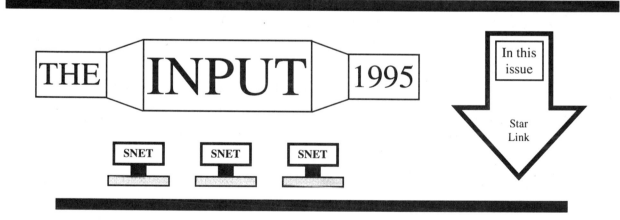

TIP: Save often.

SNET Location and SNET Membership
1. Use size 16 bold heading.
2. Use size 10 for paragraph text.

SNET Users
1. Use size 16 bold heading.
2. For paragraph text, use a two-column frame, if possible (if not, use two frames and draw a box around them). Text will flow from first to second column. Use size 10.

Star Link
1. Use a thicker border around frame as shown.
2. Use size 16 bold heading.
3. Use size 14 bold for side headings.

4. Use size 12 for other text.
5. Use bullets shown.

Logging onto Star Link
1. If available, use predrawn symbol.
2. Use size 16 bold for heading.
3. Use size 14 bold for side heading.
4. Use size 10 for other text.
5. If available, use automatic numbering command.

NEXT
1. If available, use arrow from predrawn symbols.
2. You choose font sizes.
3. Use bold style text where shown.
4. Use bullets shown.
5. Center text elements as shown.

SNET Location

SNET is now located on the XYZ-TV Star Link network. With just a microcomputer, communications software, and a modem, you will be ready to access Star Link over regular telephone lines with **no on-line charges**.

SNET Membership

With one yearly membership fee, you will have unlimited access to this communications network 24 hours a day, 365 days a year. Whenever you want to use the Net, it will be ready.

STAR LINK
Main Menu

Mail and tools

- Mail
- PBS on-line projects
- Einstein
- Student service
- Tools and utilities

Gateways

- Internet
- School news groups
- CNN newsroom
- Linkchat
- File library

Logging onto
Star Link

You can use Star Link from home, the office, or school. All you need is a log-on code and a password. An application form is included on the back of this sheet. Fill it in an mail today.

Steps to log on

1. Turn on the modem.
2. Start your communications program.
3. Dial the Star Link number.
4. Type your log-on code.
5. Type your password.
6. When the menu appears, choose your desired item.

SNET Users

If you are outside of the calling area, you will be especially glad to know that Star Link has a statewide toll-free access number.

Star Link users will also have access to the Internet, libraries, databases, and other data sources through a collection of networks around the world. You can access other educational sites in this country and participate in forums, interest groups, and discussions.

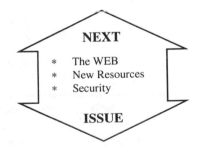

NEXT
- * The WEB
- * New Resources
- * Security

ISSUE

Directions

Shapes: Use predrawn shapes if available. **Calendar** 1. Turn on snap-to feature if available. 2. Draw the box first. 3. Zoom in (magnify).	4. Draw the lines; refer to the rulers on the top and side of the screen to help you draw the lines (suggested half-inch between lines). 5. Group the box and the lines. 6. Resize, if needed. 7. Key the days and numbers.

Your Name   Project 9

Windows

Seminar

Series

Exclusive technical
review of Windows 95

Session 1

Networking

In this session you will learn how to optimize Windows in a network. Also, you will receive tips on how to correctly set up your systems.

You'll learn new techniques for eliminating printing problems and bugs in Windows for Workgroups. You will also be given many insider tips from Novel, IBM, and Apple. This session is a must for all network managers.

Session 2

DOS Apps

Running DOS applications under Windows can be slow and problematic; some DOS applications will not print. Learn the secrets of setting up a PIF for each of your apps. Learn about PIF hot spots which most users ignore, but which cause most of their problems. Plus, our optimization clinic will show you how to modify Windows so your DOS apps fly.

Select your sessions
Shown on the right are the dates available in your city. Each day there is a six-hour session at a cost of $80 per day.

Session Times

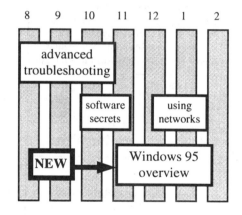

	8	9	10	11	12	1	2
		advanced troubleshooting					
				software secrets		using networks	
		NEW			Windows 95 overview		

September

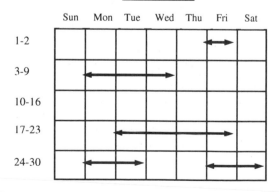

	Sun	Mon	Tue	Wed	Thu	Fri	Sat
1-2							
3-9							
10-16							
17-23							
24-30							

Directions

Font: Choose your own font sizes.	Shapes: Use predrawn shapes if available. If the shape around "Hudson Homes" is not available, draw a shape of your own design.

Your Name   Project 10

HUDSON HOMES

8.50% contract rate (8.30% APR)

Hudson Homes is introducing a new wooded development with 25 lots. Lot size varies from a half-acre to nearly one acre. The model shown on the right is a 2,550 square-foot, center-hall colonial with a two-story foyer at a list price of $215,800. It sits on a landscaped, irregular lot overlooking one of two man-made ponds.

The home's exterior of white, vinyl siding and its many windows were approved by the city architectural board. The floor plan is open, allowing an easy traffic flow between the rooms. The bayed breakfast area in the kitchen opens onto a concrete patio. Oak trim and cabinets are found throughout the home.

The two-and-a-half-car garage has a side entry, and the full basement is unfinished. The master suite on the second floor is entered through double doors, a standard feature.

model home

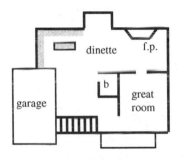

The master bedroom has five windows and a vaulted ceiling. The luxury bathroom includes a garden tub and a large, walk-in closet.

Unusual features include an art niche and plant shelf as well as skylights in the main bathroom, hardwood floors, and a window overlooking the foyer.

Great Home Loan Savings

◆ No points	◆ No closing costs
◆ No application fees	◆ No appraisal costs
◆ No title costs	◆ No up-front expenses

With only 15% down (versus 20% or more from other lenders), you avoid paying private mortgage insurance. Lower down payments are available at the same great rate.

UNIT TWO
Using Special Effects:
Color, Clip Art, and Word Art

Objectives

After completing this unit you will be able to:

- Color text and objects.
- Type white text on black text frames (text blocks).
- Use Word art (text rotation, shaded letters), and import clip art.
- Flow text between columns.
- Type paragraphs using hyphen control and justified text option.
- Overlap text frames (text blocks).
- Create border art and use special bullets.
- Overlap (wrap) graphics on text frames (text blocks).
- Type a two-page document and flow text between pages.
- Use "continued notices."
- Use character map to copy special symbols.

Your Name   Project 11

INVESTMENT ALERT

PLAN TO SAVE

FIRST NATIONAL BANK

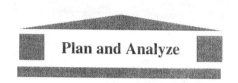

Withholding Taxes

A Gift to I.R.S. Did you know that by having too much federal income tax withheld from your paycheck you are giving Uncle Sam an interest free loan? Sure, it's nice to get a fat check back from the I.R.S after you file your tax return, but you could be earning interest on that money if it were in your savings or interest-bearing checking account.

Forced Savings. For some people, the only way they can save money for an end-of-year expense is to keep a large withholding tax. If you do not spend this money, put it in a savings account right away.

Plan and Analyze

The most important thing about investing is to make up a spending and saving plan. Chart 1 shows a spending plan for a middle-class family. This family has approximately 25% of its investment in the home, 40% in U.S. Government bonds, 30% in corporate stocks, and the rest in various savings accounts.

The second most important thing about investing is to analyze your profits on a regular basis. Chart 2 shows some fluctuation in profits. However, the trend is upward.

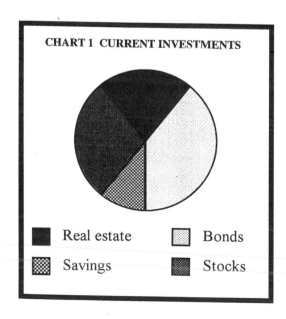

CHART 1 CURRENT INVESTMENTS

Real estate   Bonds

Savings   Stocks

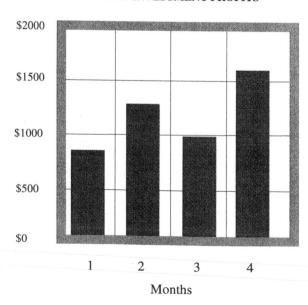

CHART 2 INVESTMENT PROFITS

Months

Font: You decide font sizes unless specified below.

Color: Use black unless other is specified below (or use all black if you are not using a color printer).

Alignment: Align or center as shown below.

Main title: Bold, all capitals; colors: green for PLAN, blue for TO, green for SAVE, yellow border.

Shapes
1. "Investment Alert" and "First National Bank": if available, use predrawn symbol.
2. "Withholding Taxes" and "Plan and Analyze": use red for the text, yellow for surrounding objects.

Paragraph text: Use size 12.

Your Name   Project 11

PLAN TO SAVE

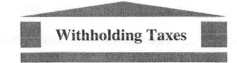

Withholding Taxes

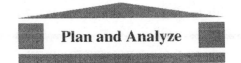

Plan and Analyze

A Gift to I.R.S. Did you know that by having too much federal income tax withheld from your paycheck you are giving Uncle Sam an interest free loan? Sure, it's nice to get a fat check back from the I.R.S after you file your tax return, but you could be earning interest on that money if it were in your savings or interest-bearing checking account.

Forced Savings. For some people, the only way they can save money for an end-of-year expense is to keep a large withholding tax. If you do not spend this money, put it in a savings account right away.

The most important thing about investing is to make up a spending and saving plan. Chart 1 shows a spending plan for a middle-class family. This family has approximately 25% of its investment in the home, 40% in U.S. Government bonds, 30% in corporate stocks, and the rest in various savings accounts.

The second most important thing about investing is to analyze your profits on a regular basis. Chart 2 shows some fluctuation in profits. However, the trend is upward.

UNIT TWO Using Special Effects

See next page for directions for bottom half of Project 11

Chart 1

1. For pie, use predrawn shape if available. If not available, draw pie with circle and lines (you may not be able to fill the slices).
2. Make each slice a different solid color. If color printer is not available, use different patterns instead of colors.
3. Use the same colors for boxes as for slices. Make boxes identical size and line up as shown. Color surrounding box in yellow.

Chart 2

1. Use thin lines for grid. Each section must be the same size.
2. Use thicker lines for surrounding box and color in yellow. Place it in front (or on top) of grid lines (use bring to front or similar command).

3. Bars must be identical widths. Use copy and paste commands. Use one color for all bars. Estimate heights. Place bars behind the surrounding box by using the send farther command, if available.
4. Line up dollar numbers on the left edge.
5. Type each month in a separate frame. Center numbers under bars. Align on bottom edge.

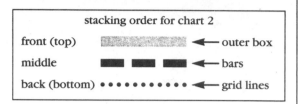

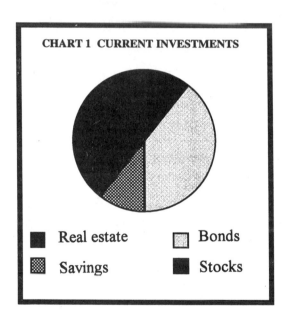

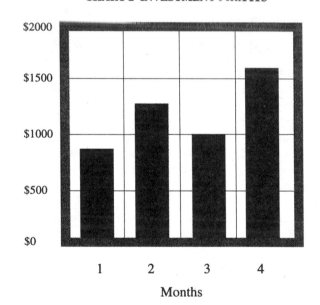

Directions

Font: You select font size unless specified.
Main title: Make bold.
"National Securities": Use white text and black shading.

Shapes
1. If available, use predrawn arrows.
2. Widths must be the same for all arrows. The heights are different.
3. Space arrows evenly.
4. Use gray shade for background and white text and black shade for numbers in arrows.
5. Center numbers (left to right) inside.
6. Center years under arrows.

"National Appreciation Fund": Use white text and black shading.
Chart on left: Each box must be the same size. Use white or black text and shading as shown.
Paragraph text: Size 12. For paragraph with note use size 10.

Bar chart
1. Bars must be the same width.
2. Space groups evenly apart.
3. Vertical scale—space numbers evenly apart.
4. Bottom scale—center numbers under the bar groups.

Legend names: Center (stocks, bonds) vertically with the boxes.

Your Name   Project 12

Looking for a stock fund with more ups than downs?

National Securities

| 1991 | 1992 | 1993 | 1994 | 1995 |
| 8% | 6% | 9% | 7% | 7% |

National Appreciation Fund

Average Annual Total Returns ended 12/31/95
27.5% (1 year)
9.25% (5 year)
7.5% (10 year)

If you're looking for a growth fund with a strong track record over the long term, consider the no-load National Appreciation Fund. Our fund has produced profits in 8 of the past 10 periods.

It has also produced double-digit average annual returns for the 10-year period that ended December 31. Numbers shown here assume that all dividends and capital gains are reinvested in any period.

Note: Past performance is no guarantee of future results. The price of shares fluctuates so much that upon redemption, a shareholder will receive more or less than the original cost.

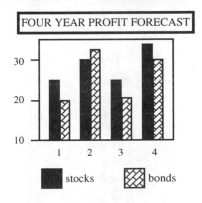

FOUR YEAR PROFIT FORECAST

stocks   bonds

The National Appreciation Fund currently gives you the opportunity to share in the growth potential for well-known companies with established brands and a large U.S. market share.

Directions

<table>
<tr>
<td>

Side title ("Computer Resource Dept.")
1. Draw frame.
2. Key words.
3. Rotate as needed.

Memo: Bold "To", "From", and "Date." Use size 12.

Paragraphs: Use size 12. Use two-column frame (ignore the disk for now).

Disk: Get from clip art (you may need Picture Frame first). Center it horizontally in text frame.

Computer: Draw computer (not clip art).

</td>
<td>

"Call soon . . ."
1. Key in text frame.
2. Use shadow (if available).
3. Overlap with drawing as shown.

"Morning schedule": Align and space items in a uniform manner. Use white on black as shown.

A Note on Clip Art
For this project and all others, select clip art that is the same or similar to that shown. This clip art is from Microsoft Publisher.

</td>
</tr>
</table>

Your Name   Project 13

COMPUTER RESOURCE DEPT.

To: Division Two Department Supervisors
From: Computer Resources Manager
Date: October 8

SUBJECT: TRAINING ON NEW WINDOWS VERSION

We have just completed upgrading our training center with the latest version of Windows and Works for Windows. Because your software will be upgraded within three months, you should plan on having your department attend training sessions as soon as possible.
Each session will cover a different topic. Topic 1 is an introduction to the new Windows operating system. Topic 2 is an in-depth look at Works word processing. Topic 3 covers Works draw tools. Topic 4 covers spreadsheets and databases. You will also have an opportunity to do a short series of learning activities and projects during a "free time" each day. An instructor will be available during these sessions to give individual help.

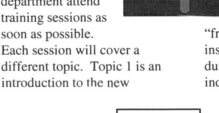

Call soon for applications

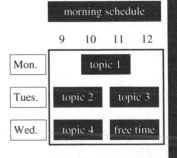

morning schedule			
9	10	11	12

	9	10	11	12
Mon.		topic 1		
Tues.	topic 2		topic 3	
Wed.	topic 4		free time	

Your Name   Project 14

Normandy Monitor

| Issue 2 | November 5 199x | A Publication of Normandy High School 2500 W. Pleasant Valley Rd. Parma, Ohio 44134 |

Scheduling

To accommodate staff needs, individual students will have access to the computer lab during lunch and activity periods only for the first month of school. Teachers may bring their classes to the lab at any prearranged time during the entire school year.

For your information, a master schedule is outside the lab. Please do not sign up on this copy; see the lab manager to reserve time.

Technology Fears

New this year, Normandy will be bringing technology closer to students and staff by offering lab and specialist assistance. This should help peel away fears that may exist regarding technology.

The lab can be utilized by teachers and their students during a regular class period. The computer resource specialist will be on hand to assist with software and equipment.

To accommodate everyone's needs, please sign up for the lab at least

one week in advance. When the lab is not being used by an entire class, students will have access to the computers during a scheduled study hall or if they have a teacher's pass.

Race in today and sign up for the sessions

Bits and Bytes

During the year, several computer-related in-service sessions will be offered to small groups. If you would prefer to work on an individual basis, time can be scheduled during your conference and planning periods or after school.

Future Connections

⇒ Communications
⇒ E-mail
⇒ World Wide Web
⇒ Internet
⇒ Gophers

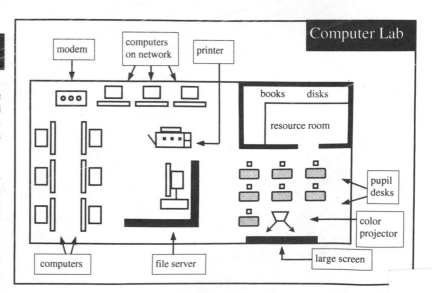

Computer Lab

modem   computers on network   printer

books   disks

resource room

pupil desks

color projector

computers   file server   large screen

Disk: If available, get from clip art.

"Issue 2": Place a text frame on top of the disk and type the words.

Date: Replace x with the current year.

"A Publication of . . ." : Use shadow.

Text paragraphs

1. Set up a separate text frame for each section approximately as shown. Allow text to flow from the bottom of the left column to the top of the middle column. The words that actually flow to the middle column probably will be different than shown.

2. Use size 10 and choose any font style.

3. Turn on the justify feature. The computer software will horizontally adjust spacing between words so that the text lines up on both the left and right.

4. Turn on the hyphenate feature. Some words at the right edge will now be hyphenated.

Car: If available, get from clip art or choose a similar picture.

"Future Connections": If available, use arrows instead of bullets.

"Computer Lab": Draw this section using drawing tools. Zoom in to do detail.

Directions

Pictures and Shapes: Get picture from clip art. If available, use predrawn shapes (if not, you may draw a box). Use a small font size to keep words inside the shapes.

Text paragraphs

1. If possible, create a single text frame.
2. Set up frame for two columns and set spacing between columns to a half-inch.

3. Use size 12.
4. Use hyphenate feature and justify.

Text frame in middle of paragraphs

1. Create a picture frame.
2. Create a slightly smaller text frame over the picture frame.
3. Use a border for the text frame only.

Your Name Project 15

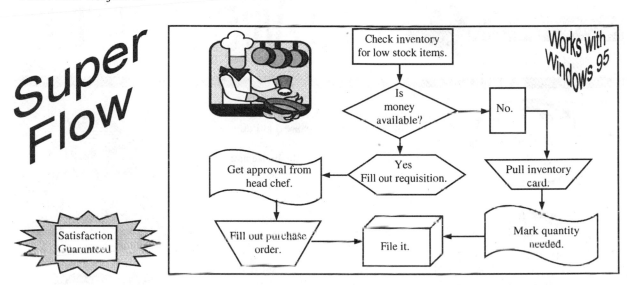

JOIN THE SUPER FLOWCHARTERS. ORDER YOUR WINDOWS 95 VERSION TODAY

Do you write job procedures, create office manuals, or make detailed job schedule steps? Have you been using a standard drawing program to create your flowcharts? If you have, then you need a flowcharting program that is both efficient and intelligent.

We have the solution to your flowcharting problems: Super Flow. It will cut your flowcharting time by 85%. It is the only intelligent flowcharter that is truly automatic. With Super Flow you can create presentation-quality flowcharts, process control diagrams, organization charts, job steps for employee manuals, and much more.

Super Flow lets you create flowcharts in less time than ever by simply keying in the information

- ◆ process flows
- ◆ job steps
- ◆ fishbone diagrams

in plain English. No drawing or graphics skills are needed. Templates are available or you can create your own templates for frequently used steps. You can use over 250 symbols that come with Super Flow or design your own with the new Symbol Editor window. Super Flow lets you change text styles, line thickness, and add special effects.

Super Flow comes with a 50-day guarantee. If you are not satisfied, return it to our closest distribution center and you will receive a prompt refund.

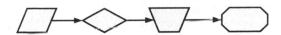

Directions

Text paragraphs: Use size 11 for text; choose any font style. **House:** Use any house from clip art gallery. **Graphic (on bottom):** Use drawing tools.	**Border art:** If available, use a border (similar to the one below) around "Sources of Indoor Air Pollution" frame. **WARNING:** This file will take a lot of disk space. Keep track of available disk space and delete old files if needed.

Your Name   Project 16

 **NEWS**

Insulation

As winter season approaches, homeowners become more concerned with reducing their utility bills. Many try to cut down on heat loss by increasing insulation in the attic and by blowing insulation into walls. While insulation is beneficial in reducing heating and cooling costs, it also traps pollution inside and reduces fresh air intake.

Carbon Monoxide

Carbon monoxide, which is odorless, can be a source of serious indoor pollution. It results from combustion from gas or propane furnaces, hot water tanks, and stoves. CO builds up in your blood and prevents your blood from carrying oxygen. In smaller amounts it can cause headaches, nausea, and vomiting. It can also be a killer. It can affect you gradually or quickly without any warning. Normally this gas is vented to the outside, but faulty equipment or clogged vents can cause a buildup inside your house. A fireplace, which pulls air from the house and sends it up the chimney, can also pull in combustion from your gas furnace. Normally, furnace combustion goes up the furnace chimney.

CO Detectors

CO detectors are now available that detect even the slightest amount of CO. These are battery driven devices that look similar to smoke detectors. They constantly monitor the air and sound an alarm if CO is detected. For the best protection, they should be located on each floor.

Sources of Indoor Air Pollution

* hair sprays
* kitchen cleaners
* cooking
* fireplace
* dust, pollen
* faulty gas stove or furnace

carbon monoxide detector

furnace

Directions

EDULINK 1. If available, use shadow option for text. 2. Use clip art for people, disk, and horse. 3. Use border art as shown (any style). 4. Draw other graphics. **Bullets:** If available, use Wingdings font for number bullets and PC. On unnumbered lines, drag indent to right as shown.	**Overlapping items:** To overlap drawn graphics in the paragraphs, you may have to create a blank picture frame. Draw items on top of picture frames. **WARNING:** This file will take a lot of disk space. Keep track of available disk space and delete old files if needed.	 ↑ drag indent to right

Your Name   Project 17

EDULINK

Electronic Information Services

 Software for all ages.

 Applications for all subjects.

 News services updated every fifteen minutes.

Low Cost and Easy to Learn

LOW COST. You can't beat the low cost of Edulink services. A $5 monthly service charge covers all services. Connect time is only $1 per hour and downloading of all software is free. While there are extensive help menus in all software packages, more detailed explanations and examples are available by purchasing software manuals. Daily updated price lists of manuals are available on Edulink.

 EASY TO LEARN. Computer novices will love Edulink. Windows compatible menus allow for easy selection of commands and help is just one click away. A help button on all screens leads the user step-by-step through all procedures.

System Requirements

★★★★★★★★★★★★★★★★★★★★★★★★★★★★
★ ❶ Personal computer with 486
★   microprocessor
★   💻 minimum 640K RAM
★   💻 DOS 5.0 or higher
★   💻 3.3 meg free space on hard disk
★   💻 VGA graphics adapter
★
★ ❷ Cable television connection
★ ❸ Edulink conversion box
★★★★★★★★★★★★★★★★★★★★★★★★★★★★

Stories, Sports, Weather

STORIES. You will receive hourly updates from two national news agencies. You will be able to read the latest breaking stories hours before you receive your local newspaper.

SPORTS and WEATHER. Results from national and local sporting events are updated every half hour. National weather forecasts and local bulletins from the National Weather Service Radio provide you with as much information as all other sources.

Directions for two-page project

TIP: Save often and make a backup.	**Text paragraphs:** Use size 12.
Headings and charts: If available, use color for main titles, title for bar chart, bars in bar chart, pie chart slices, and key.	**Pie chart:** Zoom in to make sure that the slices are attached.

Your Name   Project 18

APPLE UNIVERSITY

NEWS AND VIEWS

$3 Million Plan

The trustees have approved President Mitchel's recently submitted plan to guide the university's athletic program into the 21st century.

The plan calls for expanding Apple's tradition of success in athletics, adding resources to help student athletes excel on the playing field and in the classroom, and establishing accountability.

Under the plan, Apple will invest an additional $3 million in athletics over the next four years. This money, a loan to be paid back starting in the year 2000, will come from reserves in a facilities fund for renovating and upgrading nonacademic buildings.

This infusion of money will give Apple the biggest athletic operating budget in its ten-university conference. Mitchel told trustees in a briefing before the board vote in March that the new money would help make intercollegiate athletics self-supporting.

Expected Results

As a result of this new plan, the president and trustees expect that:

- Some university teams will be more competitive at the Division I level, gaining valuable media exposure for Apple.
- Other teams will be competitive at the regional level. (The plan includes steps for keeping Division 1-A status in football.)
- Revenues from athletics will increase through stepped-up marketing efforts, which will positively impact ticket sales, media contracts, and merchandising.

Top Four Athletic Budgets

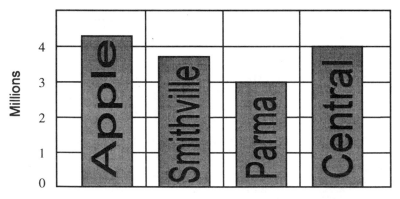

continued on next page

Opportunities for Women

Under the plan, there will be more opportunities for women in all sports. Three women's sports will be added in the next three years at a cost of $150,000 per year. This brings to 24 the number of sports offered—with an equal number for men and women to provide greater gender equity.

```
Three-Year Plan

√   Year 1        ice skating
√   Year 2        soccer
√   Year 3        golf
```

Other Improvements

There will be improved academic support for student athletes once the new plan goes into effect. Student athletes with strong educational records and financial need will be eligible to compete for fifth-year scholarships.

The old athletic center will be converted into a first-class training facility for student athletes. The center will also have a recreation area for all students, including a volleyball court, pool, weight room,

exercise room with over 100 pieces of equipment, and a short track. Students who wish to use the recreational area will pay a $100 yearly fee. This money will go for payment of bonds used to finance the center. It is estimated that it will take 30 years to pay off the bonds.

A full-time sports trainer will be available during all open hours. The trainer will help athletes to set up individual pretraining programs. A clerk will record schedules in a computer and enter dates, times, and exercises completed. Some information will be directly entered into the computer from the equipment. When leaving the center, the athlete will receive a summary of exercise results for the entire season. A daily summary will be sent to coaches.

ATHLETIC AND RECREATION CENTER

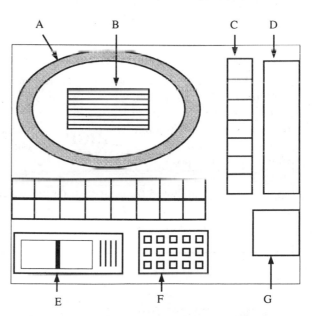

KEY TO ATHLETIC AND RECREATION CENTER

A   Four-lane track   E   Volleyball court
B   Pool with low diving   F   Exercise room
    board   G   Office and computer
C   Shower-dressing rooms   room
D   Training center

Average NCAA Budget

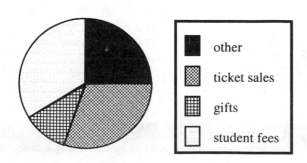

- other
- ticket sales
- gifts
- student fees

UNIT TWO   Using Special Effects

end of project

Directions for two-page project

TIP: Save often and make a backup. **Text** 1. For paragraphs use size 12. 2. Flow text between page one and two. 3. Use continued on feature if available.	**Art** 1. If available, use border art for main title (any style). 2. If available, use clip art for flags. 3. If you have separate draw software such as Works Draw, use it to draw the car. If not, use desktop publishing draw tools (use shades if available). 4. Get phone from character map, wingdings font.

Your Name   Project 19

Credit Union News

Car Sale

The CD 500

Big Selection

A special car sale for members only will occur next month. Included are domestic and foreign models such as Plymouth, Dodge, and Ford.

Everyone is a winner at National Credit Union. Join the race for new CDs, which are on sale now. The minimum deposit amount on Certificates of Deposit is just $250. This offer applies to CDs purchased for time periods of 1, 2, and 5 years. Rates are reviewed weekly to make sure that you are receiving the best rates in the city.

HIGH RATES

Take advantage of our low-minimum deposit amount and high rates before this special offer is over. The offer is for a limited time— 2 weeks from the date of this newsletter.

(Continued on page 2)

Trade-In

We will take a trade on any car or truck. Our credit union appraisers guarantee a fair appraisal.

Free Service Contract

All purchases come with a two-year service contract that covers labor and parts for all repairs. You may also purchase an extended contract for up to five years at a total

(Continued on page 2)

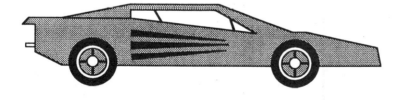

October

continued on next page

(CD 500   Continued from page 1)

You will be included, as an extra bonus, in our drawing for the following items.

☺ Kenmall 5-head VCR
☺ 40-inch Hitushe TV with PIP
☺ Planters portable computer

To purchase this CD, either stop in at the office and go to any teller or call our FAST ACTION number. You can handle everything over the phone. We will send you a deposit withdrawal form and application form. However, we will process the transaction immediately so that you receive the current interest rate. Please just return the forms to us within 5 business days and you will receive interest from the date of your phone call.

CD RATES

RATES AS OF TODAY
♥ 4% for less than 1 year
♥ 4.5% for 1 year
♥ 4.8% for over 1 year

(Service Contract   Continued from page 1) cost of only $100. The two-year contract does not cover the first month because we will replace your car with a new one during the first month if the car needs more than minor adjustments.

Also, we offer a free car rental during the first year any time you bring your car in for service. We will deliver the rental car to the location of your choice.

Special Rates

9.2%
60 months to pay
8.4%
30 months to pay

What do I do?

1 Complete the application form and mail to the Credit Union within two weeks. Our loan officer will determine the loan amount for which you are qualified and mail you a loan approval within two days.

2 Because cars will be sold on a first-come basis, be there early. If you are trading a car, be sure to bring your certificate of title.

3 If you will be getting a loan, bring five recent pay stubs and your last car insurance bill. Loan officers will be available to process loans.

AUTOMATED PHONE
Use the following codes when dialing us on a touch-tone phone.
1. Teller
2. Automated help
3. Menu
4. Account balance
5. Transfer
6. Loan information
7. Current rates
8. End the call

UNIT TWO | Using Special Effects

end of project

UNIT THREE
Creating Tables

Objectives

After completing this unit you will be able to:

- Create tables and type data.

- Merge (group) table cells to print across several columns.

- Create table borders and grids and adjust borders.

- Align data in tables and resize tables.

- Adjust width of table columns.

- Change thickness of cell borders.

- Type cell data on two lines (in the same row) and enter data in cells.

- Use "fill down."

- Change cell margins.

- Place graphic objects into cells.

Directions

Text paragraphs: Use size 12, two columns, half-inch spacing between columns. **Table** 1. Include single blank lines as shown. 2. Merge (group) cells in main title and subtitle rows so that the words print across the table (centered). 3. Use size 14 bold for main titles and column headings. 4. Use size 12 for table data. Include dollar signs and commas as shown.	5. Align word columns left, number columns right. Adjust column width for approximate uniform spacing between columns. Also, make sure that items print on single rows as shown. 6. Include a table border. **Alignment:** Center table, paragraphs, and main title between margin guides (left to right).

Your Name   Project 20

INVESTORS REPORT

If you do not have any shares in Buildco, now is the time to consider buying some. Due to high demand for quality rental properties, Buildco has been able to raise rents 2 percent above inflation this year. This has resulted in increased profits and dividends. Also, stock prices have continued to rise this year as they have during the past five years. This growth in Buildco's stock makes it worthwhile for a long-term investment. Even selling stock after a one-year period has resulted in substantial profits. We can assure you that we will continue to purchase only properties that yield above-average rental incomes. The table below shows rents that are some of the highest available.

BUILDCO PROPERTIES INCORPORATED

Rental Property Results

Building Name	Rental Agent	Square Footage	Rent Per Foot	Total Yearly Rent Due
Court Towers	Kim Sung	50,000	$25.50	$1,275,000
Medical One	Yuri Linov	24,200	$16.00	$387,200
ParmaTown	Jack Garcia	68,350	$23.50	$1,606,225
Seven Hills Plaza	Ravi Nair	120,920	$14.00	$1,692,880
Yorktown Five	Megan Flanagan	89,410	$19.00	$1,698,790
CPL Building	Atara Nelson	71,240	$18.50	$1,317,940
Brookside Center	Claude Moine	63,220	$13.00	$821,860
Columbus Park	John Nussbaum	117,900	$16.00	$1,886,400
Federal Towers	Brenda Hosokawa	84,340	$25.50	$2,150,670

Directions

Table

1. Align word columns left, number columns right. Adjust column width to avoid crowding.
2. Include border.
3. If available on your software, print grid lines as shown. You will probably have to highlight the cells first (drag mouse).

4. Include table shadow, if available.

Graphics

1. Draw truck and other graphics on bottom.
2. Use special symbols and arrows if available.
3. If star is not available, draw a circle.

Your Name   Project 21

MATTRESS SALE

SLEEP-O-MATIC
2102 Brookpark Road

- FREE removal of old bed
- FREE frame is included
- FREE installation

convenient
credit

FAST
DELIVERY

SALE PRICES NOW IN EFFECT				
OVER 50 BEDS	TWIN	FULL	QUEEN	KING
April Air	$38	$8	$17	$25
Sleep-a-pudic	$49	$10	$22	$33
Sleep All Water	$62	$12	$28	$42
Pillow Bottom	$124	$25	$56	$83
Extra Firm	$137	$27	$62	$92
Plush	$183	$37	$82	$123

Special Features

- Bunk beds
- Oak Headboards
- Johnson Brass
- Odd sizes
- Super Springs included

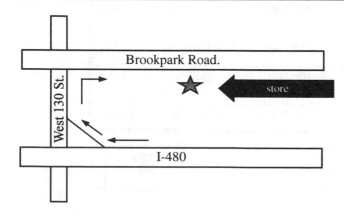

Directions

Text paragraphs: Use size 12, two columns ***Table*** 1. Use size 12. 2. Align word columns left, number columns right. Adjust column width to avoid crowding. 3. Include thicker border.	4. Include grid lines as shown. ***Graphics*** 1. Get world from clip art if available. 2. Get phone from character map. 3. Draw other objects.

Your Name   Project 22

AUTOVIEW PANELS

For Quality Projections

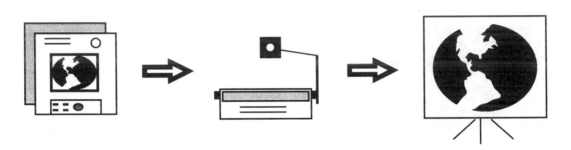

Great ideas should be projected in the best light— LCD light. Autoview is now introducing the finest quality LCD projection panels available in the world.

■ With thousands of colors and shades available, you will get brilliant full-screen projected images. Smart ideas look smarter with Autoview panels.

■ It's a snap to hook up 3 computers or video sources simultaneously. You can use a notebook, laptop, or standard PC. Big ideas look much bigger when using Autoview panels.

■ You can project onto screens up to 20 feet wide or onto a light shaded wall. Images will be crisp and clear.

DESCRIPTION	MODEL	SHADES	PANEL SIZE	PRICE
black and white panel; sound is not available	A100	500,000	7.2 inches	$800
color panel without sound	C225	850,000	8.9 inches	$1230
black and white panel (2000 shades) with sound	A101	500,000	10 inches	$960
color panel with sound	C226	900,000	12.5 inches	$1560

 Phone today for a free demonstration video.
1-800-555-8899

Directions

Text paragraphs: Use size 12. **Table** 1. Use size 12, bold where shown. 2. Align as shown. Adjust column width to avoid crowding.	3. Shut off grid lines for cells shown (you may have to highlight cells). 4. Merge (group) cells on either side of "January" and "February" in order to center these words. **Graphics:** Draw graphics and place inside cells as shown.

Your Name   Project 23

Super Scheduler

day	planned activity	start date	end date	January			February		
				5	13	20	5	13	20
1	**Product Planning**								
2	Develop ideas	1-13	2-13						
3	Make budget	1-20	2-20						
4	**Product Development**	1-5	2-5						
5	Concepts, Design	1-13	2-5						
6	Cost Analysis	2-5	2-20						
7	Marketing Plan	1-5	1-20						
8	Distribution Plan	1-5	2-20						

Simco Products now introduces Super Scheduler version 2.5. As were past versions, this software is a great way to create business and industrial schedules. It is easy to use and powerful. Everything is in one package: typing the descriptions, dates, and graphics. No drawing is necessary. You just select symbols from a pull down menu. The symbols automatically print under the correct dates.

With version 2.5, these schedules are now presentation quality. Over 50 colors are available, along with several fancy fonts. The entire schedule can be resized by simply typing in zoom percentages.

Super Schedules can be copied to other software such as word processing or graphics presentation packages. Version 2.5 will automatically track progress, revisions, and actual dates so that revised and interim schedules can be created. Schedules can be enhanced with milestones, custom bars (over 25 styles), symbols, and clip art.

Directions

Table

1. Set up one table with 7 columns and 13 rows.
2. You decide what font to use (use size 12 and larger).
3. Use light gray shading, if available, where shown.
4. Use cell merge (group) to quickly shut off vertical border lines as needed.
5. Center align bold column headings.

6. Use Fill Down, if available, for the dollar signs (table menu).
7. For squares next to "Visa," "MasterCard," and "Discover," use character map.
8. Use darker border lines as shown.

Title section: See directions below.

Use 1 row for this section. Press **ENTER key** after typing each item. Use square bullet (indents and lists).

For "purchase order," merge cells. Use large font. Center.

For company name, merge cells. Press ENTER after each word. Use white characters. Change to black shade (cursor must be inside the cell). Center it.

Your Name   Project 24

☐ Mr.			
☐ Mrs.	**PURCHASE ORDER**		**AMERICAN CANDY COMPANY**
☐ Ms.			
☐ Miss			

Please print all information.

name:

address:

city: | state: | zip:

NO.	DESCRIPTION OF ITEM	PAGE	PRICE	QUANTITY	TOTAL
			$		$
			$		$
			$		$
			$		$

CHECK PAYMENT TYPE		TOTAL ➡	$
☐ Visa ☐ MasterCard ☐ Discover		5% TAX ➡	$
		TOTAL DUE ➡	$

Directions

Text paragraphs: Use size 12. *Table* 1. For border use thicker line than grid lines. 2. Draw graphics and zoom in to do details. 3. Left align items in column 1.	4. Center the numbers in the table cells (do not use centering tool or command). Simply increase the Right Cell Margins. This will keep the numbers "right aligned" but in the center of the cells. You may be able to highlight all of the number cells before making the change.

Your Name   Project 25

KORBMAN ELECTRONICS
1500 Clocktower Ave.   Bettyville, Texas

Mrs. Ann Greenburger
Computer Manager
Sportsperson Magazine

Dear Mrs. Greenburger,

Electronic mail now permits the ready exchange of messages and computer data around the world. **EMS** (electronic mail systems) are gaining increased acceptance in most Fortune 500 corporations, particularly in large banks with international communication networks.

One of the largest users of electronic mail is IBM, where 200,000 employees use the system. This saves the company an estimated $150 million a year due to increased productivity. IBM has a system called **VNET**, which links several thousand computers worldwide.

The use of **EMS** has spread like wildfire as computer networks of all kinds become more prevalent. This has occurred due to big decreases in message cost.

COMPARISON OF MESSAGE COSTS			
mail	fax	pc	hard copy
1985	5,800	16,970	34,412	85,390

	mail	fax	pc	hard copy
1985	5,800	16,970	34,412	85,390
1986	28,233	14,500	37,900	82,411
1987	27,555	15,777	42,123	83,579
1988	37,900	25,800	37,600	85,919
Totals	119,488	73,047	152,035	337,299

Sincerely yours,

Alan Cornowski

Directions

Computer: Draw it, using shading if available. **Dog:** Use clip art if available.	**Table:** Align as shown. Center items vertically in columns 2, 3, and 4 (by changing cell margins or using vertical centering tool if available).

Your Name   Project 26

VIRUS ASSASSIN

THE ONLY SURE-FIRE ANTI-VIRUS PROGRAM

Virus Assassin is the only antivirus program that constantly monitors your modem and prevents any type of virus from infecting your computer. Have no fear. Download software from any computer worldwide. Use e-mail with any computer. Use any on-line service.

Virus Assassin automatically scans for viruses in special formats used with on-line services, e-mail sent through Internet and World Wide Web files. It also checks all files read from any floppy disk or tape drive and halts reading before any virus-infected data are stored into memory.

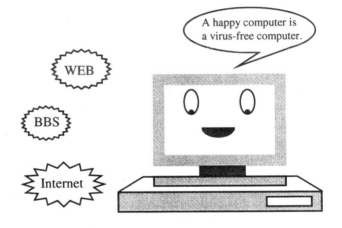

No bad bytes with Assassin

- one-button on-screen updates
- 32-bit scantron
- advanced detection technology
- low price

FEATURE COMPARISON			
Features	Assassin	Nartrons	Sickum
monitors compressed files	YES	NO	NO
checks modem activity	YES	NO	YES
monitors group folders	YES	YES	YES
checks e-mail from all sources	YES	NO	NO
checks Internet and WEB files	YES	YES	NO

Directions

Set up approximately as shown.

Your Name   Project 27

Issue 14
February

School-Net

A monthly
publication

Computer Type

Any type of MS DOS or
Windows-based computer
can be used with School-
Net. This includes
portable computers with
cell-based autolink
compatibility.

School-Net Costs			
member	basic dues	unlimited use	total dues
none	$25.50	$10.00	$35.50
School-Net	$22.25	$5.50	$27.75
Edu-Net	$23.00	$8.50	$31.50
Both	$18.25	$7.00	$25.25

Communications Software

Communications software
works with the
communications card to
direct information correctly
over the phone line. There
are commercial and public
domain communications
programs available for most
microcomputers. Prices as well
as features vary.

Modem Type

Your modem must be compatible
with your microcomputer (consult
your dealer before purchasing a
modem). You may use an internal
or external modem, but you must
have a communications card for an
external modem. School-Net
supports the following baud rates:
1200, 2400, 9600, and 14400.

Comm. Card

The communications unit (also
called a serial card or asynch
card) contains a circuit board
that allows your computer to talk
to your modem. Some
computers come with a
communications card and the
related software already
installed.

Network

A network is a group of
computers connected through
phone lines, radio signals, or
cable. A provider such as
School-Net allows the computers
to communicate with each other.

Phone Line

School-Net works on any standard
phone line for single users.
Multiple users can use System B
work group software so that up to
four lines can share one phone line.
However, a network controller is
needed for work groups.

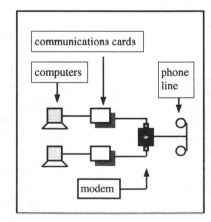

communications cards

computers

phone
line

modem

Modem Settings	
data bits	8
stop bits	2
parity	even
duplex	full
terminal	va350

UNIT THREE   Creating Tables

Directions

Coffee cup: Use clip art if available.	Symbols: Get phone, mail box, and plane from character map.

Your Name   Project 28

	ORDER FORM		mail all orders to:	Grandma's Pantry 1122 First Ave. Willville, CA 77777
gift 1	QUANTITY	ITEM NAME	CATALOG NUMBER	PRICE
	Date	Phone	Freight Total	
			Gift Total	

BREADS AND MIXES

Item no.	Description	Price
b1	Farmhouse honey bread mix	7.25
b2	Oatbran maple bread mix	6.30
b3	Buttermilk nut loaf	3.50
b4	All-bran nut and raisin mix	5.55
b5	Orange ginger scone mix	7.50
b6	Sourdough and honey loaf	3.25

credit card number

How to Order

☎ **By Phone**
Call toll free at 1-800-555-1234 during normal business hours. Sorry, we cannot accept collect calls.

✉ **By Mail**
1. Print your order and keep a copy for yourself.
2. Order by catalog gift number.
3. Please indicate arrival date. If none is specified, we will ship your order as soon as possible.
4. We reserve the right to substitute items of equal or greater value if necessary without notification.

✈ **Express Delivery**
Express air delivery for two-day service is available. Please add $5.00 per item.

Directions

Table	2. Draw graphics (use shading if available).
1. Create table as shown.	3. Use thicker lines as shown.

Your Name   Project 29

THE ELECTRONIC HOLIDAY WISH LIST

Buying china, bedspreads, furniture, and cutlery is what buying a new home meant for much of the last century. In the last ten years, electronic gadgets have become the primary focus of new home buyers. Much more interest has been shown in buying videocassette recorders, cordless telephones, compact disc players, answering machines, and computers.

Spending on electronics has increased by 44% since 1980, which is 1.6% now compared to 1.1% in 1980. Approximately $54 billion was spent on electronics in 1989. Spending on furniture has remained pretty steady, at 5% of total consumer spending. Spending on clothing has dropped 6%. Spending on food has dropped 3%.

Many electronic devices are now common in the home. For example, about 70% of homes have VCRs now compared to 17% in 1985. There are several reasons for this. First, the prices of many electronic products have dropped to the level that the average person can afford them. This is the result of increased competition which causes prices to drop. Secondly, many new uses of electronics have been found such as electronic mail, fax, improved video games, and automated teller machines.

Sales in Thousands

	answering machines	computers	televisions	compact discs
500			■	
400	■		■	⊗
300	■	▭	■	⊗
200	■	▭	■	⊗
100	■	▭	■	⊗

UNIT FOUR
Importing OLE Composition and Layout

Objectives

After completing this unit you will be able to:

- Import word processing text.

- Compose a resume.

- Import spreadsheets.

- Import charts.

- Compose a school newspaper.

- Compose a house sale flyer.

- Use OLE embedding techniques.

- Given raw data, design, layout, and create a report.

Directions

Use your word processor, not the publisher, to key what is shown below. Save it. **Print** to paper. Do not hand in now. Hand in later with the sheet printed using the publisher. This is proof that you used a word processor to create the text (rather than to type it in the publisher). **Copy** the paragraphs. Then **paste** them to the window (see next page).	For paragraphs, use size 12. Bold all headings. Add main heading and clip art (bird) to top of the window. **Drawing on bottom:** Either use drawing tools or other drawing software (copy and paste).

Your Name   Project 30   page 1

March Meeting

The March meeting will be at the Rocky River Nature Center on the Valley Parkway in North Olmsted. Sue Smith, who has recently completed her graduate work at John Carroll University, will talk about her studies of local Great Blue Heron Colonies. Her presentation is entitled, "What is a Good Home for a Great Blue Heron?"

March Field Trip

In conjunction with our program topic this month, John Romano will lead a trip to Pinery Narrows to see the Great Blue Herons return to their nesting area. On Sunday, March 26, we will meet at the Station Rd. Bridge parking area off Riverview Rd. in the Brecksville Reservation. See the map below.

The Endangered Species Act

The Endangered Species Coalition is sponsoring a Medicine Bottle Campaign designed to show Congress that we want to save potential medicines by saving today's plants and animals. Nearly one fourth of the medicines prescribed in the U.S. are based on substances derived from nature.

The Madagascar periwinkle provides a compound that is used to treat leukemia, and the bark of the Pacific yew yields Taxoi, which is used to treat ovarian and breast cancer. No one knows how many other beneficial compounds are waiting to be found. In the meantime, entire ecosystems are disappearing, and it's possible that the sources of new drugs could disappear before we even discover them.

Please voice your concern about the Endangered Species Act by attaching the labels below to empty medicine bottles and sending them to your representatives in Congress.

continued on next page

Your Name   Project 30   page 2

Cuyahoga Valley
Audubon Society

March Meeting

The March meeting will be at the Rocky River Nature Center on the Valley Parkway in North Olmsted. Sue Smith, who has recently completed her graduate work at John Carroll University, will talk about her studies of local Great Blue Heron Colonies. Her presentation is entitled, "What is a Good Home for a Great Blue Heron?"

March Field Trip

In conjunction with our program topic this month, John Romano will lead a trip to Pinery Narrows to see the Great Blue Herons return to their nesting area. On Sunday, March 26, we will meet at the Station Rd. Bridge parking area off Riverview Rd. in the Brecksville Reservation. See the map below.

The Endangered Species Act

The Endangered Species Coalition is sponsoring a Medicine Bottle Campaign designed to show Congress that we want to save potential medicines by saving today's plants and animals. Nearly one fourth of the medicines prescribed in the U.S. are based on substances derived from nature.

The Madagascar periwinkle provides a compound that is used to treat leukemia, and the bark of the Pacific yew yields Taxoi, which is used to treat ovarian and breast cancer. No one knows how many other beneficial compounds are waiting to be found. In the meantime, entire ecosystems are disappearing, and it's possible that the sources of new drugs could disappear before we even discover them.

Please voice your concern about the Endangered Species Act by attaching the labels below to empty medicine bottles and sending them to your representatives in Congress.

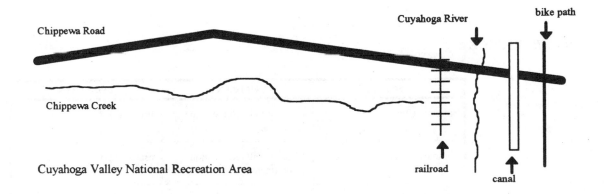

Chippewa Road

Chippewa Creek

Cuyahoga Valley National Recreation Area

Cuyahoga River

bike path

railroad

canal

end of project

Directions

Compose a personal resume for yourself. Shown below is an example, but you do not have to follow this format. Refer to other sources such as a typing or	English text, sources at your library, etc. Be sure to spell check.

Your Name   Project 31

Mary Doe
123 Red Avenue
Pleasant Falls, Texas 12366
(216) 888-7777

PRIOR EDUCATION

Graduated from Pleasant Falls Junior High School, 3.5 grade average

CURRENT EDUCATION

School: Pleasant Falls High School
                 601 Smart Street
                 Pleasant Falls, Texas 12366
Year: Junior

Current Classes: Biology 201, English 305, Advanced Computers, Business Law

Special Classes: **Computers**: word processing, spreadsheets, charting, database, desktop publishing, graphics

                 Business: typing (50 words per minute), accounting, management, sales

Activities: **Cheerleading**: squad leader, helped create cheers and dance routines, organized fund-raising activities

                 Student government: on curriculum advisory panel, student court, planned school dances

Current grade: 3.2 grade-point average first semester, absent 2 days

REFERENCES

James Snipity: Teacher, Pleasant Falls High School, 601 Smart Street, Pleasant Falls, Texas 12366, 888-1111
Carol Tennisburt: Supervisor, T-Mart, 505 Main Street, Pleasant Falls, Texas 12366, 888-2222

JOB EXPERIENCE

DATES	COMPANY	POSITION
summer 19xx	Pleasant Falls Recreation Department	life guard
summer 19xx	Pleasant Falls Recreation Department	assistant pool supervisor
Sept. 19xx to May 19xx	T-Mart	sales, sports department

See directions on next page

Your Name   Project 32

NO-WASTE RECYCLE COMPANY

The following summary shows that revenues have been steadily increasing during the year. Considering the uncertain economic times, the company continued to show profits as it has over the past five years.

Revenue by Product The main reason for revenue increases during the year was an increase in collections. Paper collections were low last year, but paper brought in the most revenue and profit for the company this year. Also, costs for processing paper declined because of new equipment purchased last year.

Revenue	Q1	Q2	Q3	Q4	TOTAL
Glass	$45,666.00	$75,300.00	$41,850.00	$68,000.00	$X
Paper	$61,649.00	$101,655.00	$56,497.00	$91,800.00	$X
Metal	$36,780.00	$25,900.00	$39,000.00	$22,000.00	$X
Plastic	$67,675.00	$47,656.00	$71,760.00	$40,480.00	$X
Totals	$X	$X	$X	$X	$X

Revenue Analysis

The bar chart on the right shows revenue for the four main waste materials that our company processes. The revenue increases indicate that cities are building their recycling programs beyond just collecting glass and paper. Revenue from metal and plastic have increased as their programs have

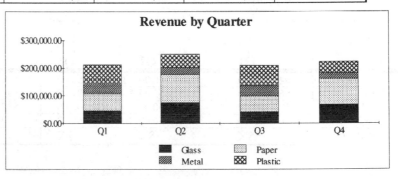

gained volume. However, there still is price pressure as the supply of recyclable materials continues to exceed demand. Much needs to be done to find new ways to use these materials. This will increase demand and prices and provide an incentive for cities to recycle even more types of materials.

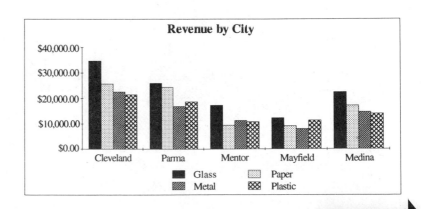

continued on next page

47

Directions

Getting Started
1. Start up a page.
2. Key in the title and first two paragraphs (see previous page).
3. Save.

Spreadsheet 1
1. Start up your spreadsheet software (not the desktop publishing program).
2. Create the spreadsheet shown below. Replace x's with calculated values and column totals.

3. Totals: add four previous columns.
4. Save the spreadsheet (do not print).
5. Copy and paste spreadsheet as table data (new table) to the window (steps will vary depending on software).
6. Align "revenue" column on the left. Align the other columns on the right.
7. Change the font to Times New Roman.
8. Use bold and thicker border line as shown.
9. Save the file now.

Spreadsheet 1

Revenue	Q1	Q2	Q3	Q4	TOTAL
Glass	$45,666.00	$75,300.00	$41,850.00	$68,000.00	$X
Paper	$61,649.00	$101,655.00	$56,497.00	$91,800.00	$X
Metal	$36,780.00	$25,900.00	$39,000.00	$22,000.00	$X
Plastic	$67,675.00	$47,656.00	$71,760.00	$40,480.00	$X
Totals	$X	$X	$X	$X	$X

Revenue	Q1	Q2	Q3	Q4	TOTAL
Glass	$45,666.00	$75,300.00	$41,850.00	$68,000.00	$X
Paper	$61,649.00	$101,655.00	$56,497.00	$91,800.00	$X
Metal	$36,780.00	$25,900.00	$39,000.00	$22,000.00	$X
Plastic	$67,675.00	$47,656.00	$71,760.00	$40,480.00	$X
Totals	$X	$X	$X	$X	$X

table as it will appear on the page
(x's represent values that should print)

continued on next page

Directions

Third paragraph
1. Set up a text frame the width of the page.
2. Key the heading and third paragraph (revenue analysis, see first page).
3. Save.

Bar chart 1
1. Create and save the bar chart from the spreadsheet software.

2. Use a solid pattern and different color for each series for output to a color printer. (Use black with a different pattern for each series for output to a non-color printer.)
3. Copy the bar chart.
4. Paste bar chart to the window.
5. Resize the bar chart so that it covers about 2/3 of the page, left to right.

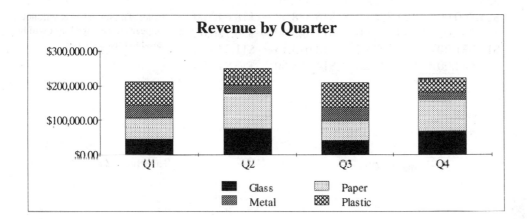

Bar chart 1

continued on next page

Directions

Spreadsheet 2 and Bar chart 2

1. Create and save the spreadsheet shown below (it will *not* be placed on the page).
2. Create and save the bar chart from spreadsheet.
3. Use a solid pattern and different color for each series for output to a color printer. (Use black with a dif-ferent pattern for each series for output to a non-color printer.)
4. Copy the chart.
5. Paste the chart onto the page.
6. Resize the chart so that it covers about 2/3 of the page, left to right.

	Glass	Paper	Metal	Plastic
Cleveland	$34,650.00	$25,641.00	$22,522.50	$21,483.00
Parma	$25,890.00	$24,336.60	$16,828.50	$18,640.80
Mentor	$17,300.00	$9,342.00	$11,245.00	$10,726.00
Mayfield	$12,331.00	$9,124.94	$8,015.15	$11,344.52
Medina	$22,444.00	$17,147.22	$14,588.60	$13,915.28

Spreadsheet 2

note: The spreadsheet will not appear on the page but it will be used to create chart 2.

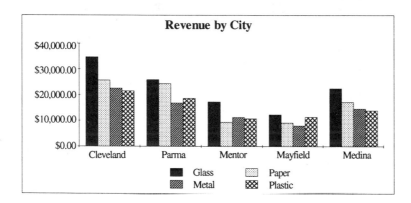

Bar chart 2

end of project

50

Project 33 SCHOOL NEWSPAPER

This project involves composing your own school newspaper. It will be two pages long and include articles, an advertisement, clip art or graphics, word art, and border art. You will compose all articles.

Directions

Setup requirements

1. Length of newspaper is two pages. Longer articles may be continued on page two (use "continued on and from" option).
2. Use a 3 column layout for text.
3. For paragraph text use size 10 Times New Roman or similar font that is easy to read.
4. Use a 1/2 to 3/4 inch page margin area.
5. If a color printer is available, use black for paragraphs, other colors for titles, headings, etc.

Content requirements

1. For main heading area (2 inch maximum height) include newspaper name, date, small graphic or clip art, and border art.

2. Include a title for each article. Graphics or pictures are not needed. If you decide to include a graphic or picture for an article, it must not exceed 2″ by 2″. The subject matter must be appropriate for school.
3. Include one advertisement per page. Get ideas from newspapers, magazines, etc. Include text and graphics or clip art. Maximum size 3″ by 3″.

Article suggestions: School events, sports, review of a play, interview with a student, trips, fund raising, club events, editorial, jobs available for students. You can include true information about your school or you can make it up.

Saving: Be sure to check the Backup Box when saving.

Printing: Make a daily printing so that your teacher can check your progress.

This project involves composing a one-page flyer for the sale of a house. It will include a description of the features, room layout, and map of the house.

Directions

Setup requirements

1. Length of flyer is one page minimum.
2. Create your own layout.
3. For paragraph text use size 10 Times New Roman or similar font that is easy to read.
4. Use a 1/2 to 3/4 inch page margin area.
5. If a color printer is available, use black for paragraphs, other colors for titles, headings, etc.

Paragraph requirements

1. Describe location and community (i.e., name of city, description of schools, parks, recreation, shopping, fire department, communication events).
2. Describe exterior of house including lot (i.e., house style, condition of roof, landscaping).
3. Describe rooms (i.e., number of rooms, estimated sizes, good points such as fireplace, natural wood).
4. Describe recent improvements (i.e., roof, heating, painting, lighting fixtures).

Other requirements

1. Draw a map to the house. Show how to get to the house from major roads.
2. Draw a layout of each floor. Label each room. Include windows, doors, stairs. You may include other features as desired. Shown below is an example of a room layout—do not use this.

Using OLE (Object Linking and Embedding)

Introduction

This is an explanation of a special software procedure called OLE (Object Linking and Embedding), that may be available on your software. If you do not have OLE, you can still do the projects in this section. OLE just makes it easier to place other objects, such as spreadsheets onto your page. You will only be using the embedding for these projects, not the linking.

OLE is a standard software technique that is found on many different types of software such as word processing, spreadsheets, and desktop publishing. You may have already used embedding without realizing it.

For example, if you ever pasted a paint graphic into a word processing file, you may have been able to double click the graphic to modify it right on the word processing screen. This is embedding. This would have saved you from starting the original paint software and then opening the paint file.

Embedding

There are two methods of embedding an object. Method One, as shown below, involves starting from the original software. Method Two involves creating the graphic right from the word processor.

Embedding Method One. In this method you must start up the paint software separately. You may, if you like, save the original paint file on disk as you normally would. When you later save the word processing file to disk, it will include the paint graphic with it. This is separate from the original paint file.

Embedding Method Two. In this method, you just start up one program, the word processor. You type the paragraphs as usual. When you are ready to create the graphic, just use the Insert Paint command (or similiar command). This will bring a paint window on the screen. After you create the graphic, "exit" the paint window and the graphic will be on the word processing screen. To make changes in the graphic, just double click it and the paint window will return.

Linking

Linking works similiar to embedding. However, with linking there is always a separate source file that contains the object. The source file is "linked" with the object in the other file so that any time a change is made in either file, both are updated automatically.

Note: The examples on this page use a paint and word processing screen, but embedding works on other software including most publishing software.

Embedding Method 1

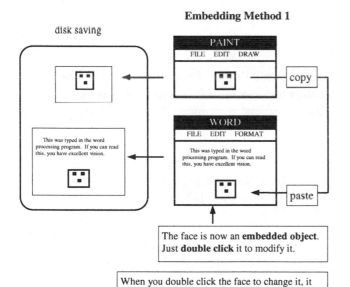

The face is now an **embedded object**. Just **double click** it to modify it.

When you double click the face to change it, it will only change the embedded face on the word processing screen. The original face on the Paint window will not be changed.

Embedding Method 2

1 Start paint window right from word processing window

2 Create the graphic. Then "exit" the paint window.

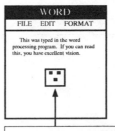

3 After exiting paint, the graphic is placed onto the word processing page.

Hint: save the word processing page right away. Otherwise you could accidentally erase the graphic.

The face is now an **embedded object**. Just **double click** it to modify it.

This project involves integrating word processing, a spreadsheet, a graphic, and desktop publishing. If you do not have spreadsheet software, you may create the information in a table. The following is a summary of what you will do.

1. Type the letter without the graphics or spreadsheet.
2. Create the spreadsheet.
3. Create the page: draw the graphic on the page, copy and paste (or import) the letter onto the page, and copy and paste (embed) the spreadsheet onto the page.

Directions

TIP: Save often and make a backup.

Create the letter

1. Start up a new word processing screen.
2. Maximize the word processing screen to give you plenty of working room.
3. You decide what fonts and sizes to use.

4. Replace the date with current month, day, and year.
5. Make sure that all words are correct.
6. Make sure that spacing and blank lines are correct.
7. Check spelling.
8. Save (use W35 as the file name).

May 4, 19xx

Mrs. Maria Marcellio
Marcellio Pizza Inc.
123 Main St.
Chesterville, California 71294

Dear Mrs. Marcellio:

Thank you for continuing to support our booster club. Shown below is the sales report that you requested. This month's sales are about 10% greater than last month. The boosters brochure that you have been placing in your take-out orders has helped make people aware of our hat sales.

Please send us the coupon packets for the pizza specials. Because we will issue one packet to each customer, please send us 1000 packets. That should be enough supply for over one month. Issuing of coupons should benefit your business as well as the booster club.

Sincerely,

continued on next page

54

Directions

Create the spreadsheet

1. Start up a new spreadsheet (start up a separate spreadsheet program)
2. Maximize the spreadsheet to give you plenty of working room.
3. You decide what fonts and sizes to use.
4. For calculations see directions in separate box below.

5. Format for dollar signs (2 decimal places).
6. Adjust column width to eliminate crowding.
7. Align (see directions below).
8. Center main title.
9. Check spelling.
10. Save right now using S35 as the file name.

---

total sales
quantity sold times sales price
You should get $6875.00 for hats.

sales tax
.07 times total sales
You should get $481.25 for hats.

total collected
total sales plus sales tax
You should get $7356.25 for hats.

BOOSTER CLUB SALES

SALES ITEM	QUANTITY SOLD	SALES PRICE	TOTAL SALES	SALES TAX	TOTAL COLLECTED
hats	550	$12.50	$x.xx	$x.xx	$x.xx
shirts	123	$4.25	$x.xx	$x.xx	$x.xx
mugs	74	$5.00	$x.xx	$x.xx	$x.xx
socks	178	$3.85	$x.xx	$x.xx	$x.xx
totals			$x.xx	$x.xx	$x.xx
left	right	right	right	right	right

continued on next page

Directions

Create the page	
1. Start a new screen. Type your name and project number.	5. Copy the spreadsheet.
2. Draw the graphics for the top of the letter shown below.	6. Paste the spreadsheet (as an object—this embeds it) onto the page, under the letter. If you need to change it later, just double click it.
3. Save now using P35 as the file name. Be sure to make a backup, if possible.	7. Spell check and print.
4. Paste (or import) the letter under the graphic.	8. Shown below is approximately how the final result should look (x's represent numbers that should print).

Your Name   Project 35

 Chesterville Booster Club

185 Forrest Wood Drive
Chesterville, California 71294

May 4, 19xx

Mrs. Maria Marcellio
Marcellio Pizza Inc.
123 Main St.
Chesterville, California 71294

Dear Mrs. Marcellio:

Thank you for continuing to support our booster club. Shown below is the sales report that you requested. This month's sales are about 10% greater than last month. The boosters' brochure that you have been placing in your take-out orders has helped make people aware of our hat sales.

Please send us the coupon packets for the pizza specials. Because we will issue one packet to each customer, please send us 1000 packets. That should be enough supply for over one month. Issuing of coupons should benefit your business as well as the Booster Club.

Sincerely,

BOOSTER CLUB SALES

SALES ITEM	QUANTITY SOLD	SALES PRICE	TOTAL SALES	SALES TAX	TOTAL COLLECTED
hats	550	$12.50	$x.xx	$x.xx	$x.xx
shirts	123	$4.25	$x.xx	$x.xx	$x.xx
mugs	74	$5.00	$x.xx	$x.xx	$x.xx
socks	178	$3.85	$x.xx	$x.xx	$x.xx
totals			$x.xx	$x.xx	$x.xx

end of project

Project 36 BUSINESS REPORT

This project involves integrating word processing, a spreadsheet, a bar chart (created from the spreadsheet), a graphic, and desktop publishing. The following is a summary of what you will do.

1. Start a screen and draw the graphic.
2. Create the spreadsheet (possibly directly from the page).
3. Put the spreadsheet onto the page.
4. Type the paragraph directly on the screen.
5. Create a bar chart from the spreadsheet data.
6. Put (embed) the bar chart onto the page.

Directions

TIP: Save often and make a backup.

Draw the graphic

1. Start a new screen. Type your name and project number.

2. Draw the graphics for the top of the letter as shown below.

3. Save now using P36 as the file name. Be sure to make a backup, if possible.

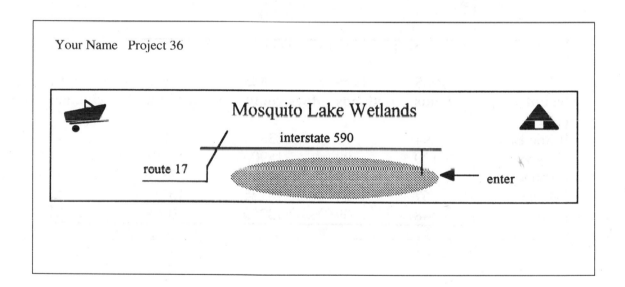

continued on next page

Directions

Create the spreadsheet

1. Start up a new spreadsheet (either start up a separate spreadsheet program or you may be able to do it directly from your publishing software).
2. Maximize the spreadsheet to provide plenty of working room. Hint: If you start the spreadsheet right from the screen, you may have to drag a border to make the window larger (try sides or corners).
3. Create the spreadsheet approximately as shown.
4. You decide what fonts and sizes to use.
5. Calculation: Duck Count Change: 1985 count–1995 count (you should get 1297 for Little Bend).
6. If you started up a separate spreadsheet software, save right now using S36 as the file name.

Embed the spreadsheet

If you created the spreadsheet directly on the window:

1. Exit the spreadsheet (and Update). This will embed the spreadsheet onto the page.
2. Save the screen immediately (still P36).

If you created the spreadsheet by starting the spreadsheet software separately:

1. Copy the spreadsheet (you may have to shut off grid lines and then highlight it first).
2. Paste it to the screen as an object (this will embed it).
3. Save the screen now (still P36).

If you need to change the spreadsheet later, just double click it.

ENVIRONMENTAL IMPACT REPORT					
county	1985 wetlands	1995 wetlands	1985 duck count	1995 duck count	duck count change
Little Bend	94	77	23870	22573	x
Dogwood	120	98	16900	15858	x
Orange	85	69	28500	23370	x
Maple	67	54	18725	15354	x
Cedar	48	39	13250	10999	x

continued on next page

Directions

Key the paragraphs
1. Key the paragraphs directly on the screen.
2. Spell check.
3. You decide what fonts and sizes to use.

4. Save now.
5. Shown below is approximately how the project should look so far (x's represent numbers that should print).

ENVIRONMENTAL IMPACT REPORT				
county	**1985 wetlands**	**1995 wetlands**	**1985 duck count**	**1995 duck count**	**duck count change**
Little Bend	94	77	23870	22573	x
Dogwood	120	98	16900	15858	x
Orange	85	69	28500	23370	x
Maple	67	54	18725	15354	x
Cedar	48	39	13250	10999	x

Shown here is a summary of recent research of wetlands in a five county area of the state. Farmers have continued to eliminate small- to medium-size ponds by adding fill dirt. However, much of wetlands destruction has occurred in suburban areas where housing developments are expanding. This has resulted in a decrease in nesting habitat for ducks and for many other bird species. The chart below shows a direct relationship between wetlands and duck counts.

continued on next page

Directions

Create the bar chart

If you created the spreadsheet directly on the window:

1. On the screen, copy the spreadsheet.
2. On the screen, paste the spreadsheet (as an object). You will now see two identical spreadsheets.
3. Double click the second spreadsheet.
4. Increase the window size and create the bar chart as shown below from the spreadsheet data.

If you created the chart from a separate spreadsheet file:

1. Open the spreadsheet file if not already opened.
2. Create the bar chart as shown below from the spreadsheet data.
3. Save it (still S36).

Embed the bar chart

If you created the chart directly on the window:

1. Exit the chart (and Update). This will embed the chart onto the page.
2. Save the screen immediately (still P36).
3. Spell check and print.

If you created the chart from a separate spreadsheet file:

1. Copy the chart.
2. Paste it to the screen (as an object—this embeds it).
3. Save the screen now (still P36).
4 Spell check and print.

If you need to change the spreadsheet later, just double click it.

The vertical scale numbers may be different on your chart.

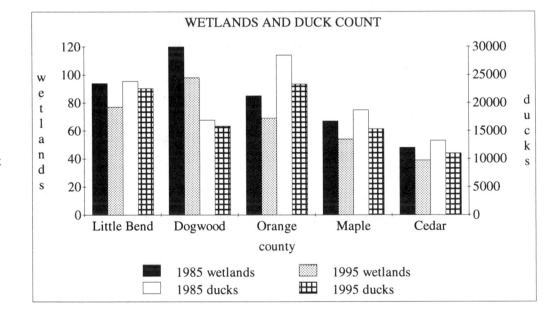

continued on next page

Shown below is approximately how the final result should look (x's represent numbers that should print).

	1985 wetlands	1995 wetlands	1985 duck count	1995 duck count	duck count change
ENVIRONMENTAL IMPACT REPORT					
county					
Little Bend	94	77	23870	22573	x
Dogwood	120	98	16900	15858	x
Orange	85	69	28500	23370	x
Maple	67	54	18725	15354	x
Cedar	48	39	13250	10999	x

Shown here is a summary of recent research of wetlands in a five-county area of the state. Farmers have continued to eliminate small- to medium-size ponds by adding fill dirt. However, much of wetlands destruction has occurred in suburban areas where housing developments are expanding. This has resulted in a decrease in nesting habitat for ducks and for many other bird species. The chart below shows a direct relationship between wetlands and duck counts.

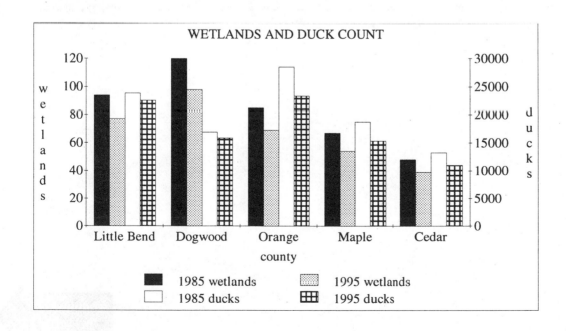

This project involves integrating word processing, a spreadsheet, a bar chart (created from the spreadsheet), graphics added to the bar chart, and desktop publishing. The following is a summary of what you will do.

1. Start a screen and type the main titles and the paragraph directly on the screen.
2. Create the spreadsheet (possibly directly from the page).
3. Put the spreadsheet onto the page.
4. Create a bar chart from the spreadsheet data and add graphics.
5. Put the bar chart onto the page and draw the graphics.

Directions

TIP: Save often and make a backup.

Key the paragraphs

1. Key the titles and paragraphs directly on the screen in two columns.

2. Spell check.
3. You decide which fonts and sizes to use.
4. Save using P37 as the file name.
5. Shown below is how the project should look so far.

Your Name   Project 37

ENVIRONMENTAL REPORT

Results. Over 100 biology students from twenty schools participated in the survey. Counts were taken in the field over a one-month period in five states. Students were assigned specific areas to survey to prevent duplication. Survey sheets were sent to the National Audubon Society, which compiled the results and sent the raw data to all participating schools.

continued on next page

Directions

Create the spreadsheet

1. Start up a new spreadsheet (either start up a separate spreadsheet program or you may be able to do it directly from your publishing software).
2. Maximize the spreadsheet to provide plenty of working room. Hint: If you start the spreadsheet right from the screen, you may have to drag a border to make the window larger (try sides or corners).
3. Create the spreadsheet approximately as shown.
4. You decide what fonts and sizes to use.
5. Calculation: Total: add the 3 previous columns.
6. If you started up separate spreadsheet software, save right now using S37 as the file name.

Embed the spreadsheet

If you created the spreadsheet directly on the window:

1. Exit the spreadsheet (and Update). This will embed the spreadsheet onto the page.
2. Save the screen immediately (still P37).

If you created the spreadsheet by starting the spreadsheet software separately:

1. Copy the spreadsheet (you may have to shut off grid lines and then highlight it first).
2. Paste it to the screen as an object (this will embed it).
3. Save the screen now (still P37).

If you need to change the spreadsheet later, just double click it.

GROUP 1 TREE SURVEY RESULTS

tree types	saplings	mature	dead	total
Willow Oak	1755	2457	877	x
Prairic Sumac	1422	1990	711	x
Sassafras	2147	3005	1073	x
Hackberry	955	1337	477	x
Blackjack Oak	1360	1904	680	x
Total				x

use thick border

continued on next page

Directions

Create the bar chart

If you created the spreadsheet directly on the window:
1. On the screen, copy the spreadsheet.
2. On the screen, paste the spreadsheet (as an object). You will now see two identical spreadsheets.
3. Double click the second spreadsheet.
4. Increase the window size and create the bar chart as shown below from the spreadsheet data.

If you created the chart from a separate spreadsheet file:
1. Open the spreadsheet file if not already opened.
2. Create the bar chart as shown below from the spreadsheet data.
3. Save it (still S37).

Embed the bar chart

If you created the chart directly on the window:
1. Exit the chart (and Update). This will embed the chart onto the page.
2. Save the screen immediately (still P37).

If you created the chart from a separate spreadsheet file:
1. Copy the chart.
2. Paste it to the screen (as an object—this embeds it).
3. Save the screen now (still P37).

Graphics: Draw the symbols on top of the bars of the chart. You may not be able to shade them. See the next page for the graphics.

If you need to change the spreadsheet later, just double click it.

The vertical scale numbers may be different on your chart.

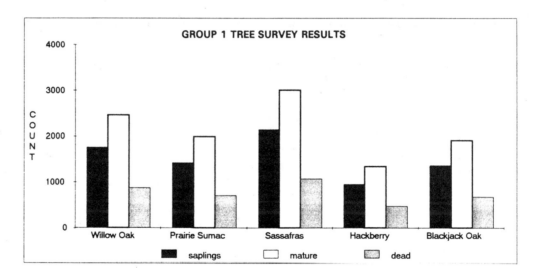

continued on next page

Shown below is approximately how the final result should look (x's represent numbers that should print).

Your Name   Project 37

ENVIRONMENTAL REPORT

Results. Over 100 biology students from twenty schools participated in the survey. Counts were taken in the field over a one-month period in five states. Students were assigned specific areas to survey to prevent duplication.

Survey sheets were sent to the National Audubon Society, which compiled the results and sent the raw data to all participating schools.

GROUP 1 TREE SURVEY RESULTS

tree types	saplings	mature	dead	total
Willow Oak	1755	2457	877	5089
Prairie Sumac	1422	1990	711	4123
Sassafras	2147	3005	1073	6225
Hackberry	955	1337	477	2769
Blackjack Oak	1360	1904	680	3944
Total				22150

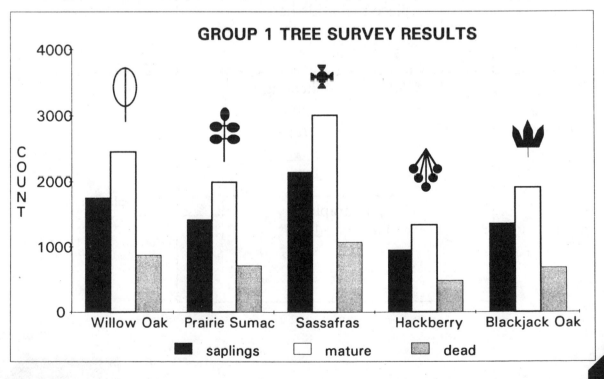

GROUP 1 TREE SURVEY RESULTS

UNIT FOUR   OLE Composition and Layout

end of project

In this project, you will make most of the design decisions. General layout suggestions are given below for the two-page report. Color may be used. The raw data is given on the following pages.

Required: Add one clip art image of your choice and at least one use of word art or special word effects.

Design Tip

Fonts. You may use different fonts and sizes but avoid using more than 2 fonts and 3 sizes. Too many changes can make it distracting.

Placement. Don't crowd objects.

Color. If you choose to use color, do not use too many colors.

page 1 layout

```
place main title here

paragraph        spreadsheet
1                Reduce it down so that
                 it fits.  Use small font
paragraph        size if needed.
2

line chart

Reduce it down so that it fits.  Use small
font size if needed.
```

page 2 layout

```
place main title here

paragraph 4        heating
Purpose            phase
                   graphic
clip

paragraph 3
(lab procedure)
```

place in two columns

continued on next page

Shown below on this page and the next page is the data that will be included. It will not look this way when placed on your page.

CHEMISTRY 101   LAB REPORT   page 1 of 2

title page 1

CHEMISTRY 101   LAB REPORT   page 2 of 2

title page 2

Results. This lab experiment shows the effects of gradually adding heat and removing heat from acetamide. A point is reached where a phase change occurs and the solid turns to liquid. Temperatures and observations were made at various time intervals. The data below shows that during heating, acetamide is totally liquid at 82.5 degrees (centigrade). During cooling, it becomes completely solid at 76.2 degrees.

paragraph 1

Data Analysis. A spreadsheet was used to store the results. A chart was then created by using the spreadsheet data. This information was then copied to a word processing document to create this report.

paragraph 2

Lab Procedure. Proper safety procedures were used including the wearing of goggles, apron, and gloves. A ring stand was set up with a beaker holder placed one foot from the bottom. A beaker with water was placed on the beaker stand. A test tube with acetamide was clamped two feet above the bottom, positioned above the beaker. A thermometer was placed into the test tube. To heat the water, a gas burner was placed below the beaker.

paragraph 3

Purpose. The purpose of this lab experiment is to determine the melting point of acetamide.

paragraph 4

LAB RESULTS AND OBSERVATIONS

time	temp.	observation	temp.	observation
		heating phase		cooling phase
0	32.0	totally solid	87.0	all liquid
15	37.5	milky	84.5	odor present, clear
30	42.2	milky	82.2	odor present, clear
45	74.6	milky	81.2	solidification begins
60	80.2	crystals melting	80.9	less odor present
75	80.9	odor present	80.9	no odor present
90	80.9	odor present	80.9	no odor present
105	80.9	most crystals melted	80.9	no odor present
120	82.5	totally liquid	80.9	no odor present
135	84.0	clear	80.9	no odor present
150	86.8	clear	80.9	no odor present
165	89.8	clear	80.9	no odor present
180	92.0	bubbles	80.5	crystallized

spreadsheet

Use left alignment for all columns.

Format temp columns for one decimal place.

Use data here for creating line chart.

continued on next page

Shown below is the data that will be included. It will not look this way when placed on your publisher page.

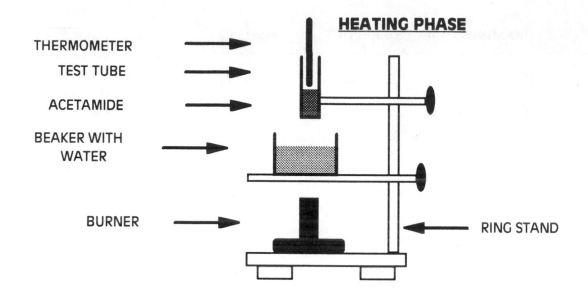

HEATING PHASE

THERMOMETER

TEST TUBE

ACETAMIDE

BEAKER WITH WATER

BURNER

RING STAND

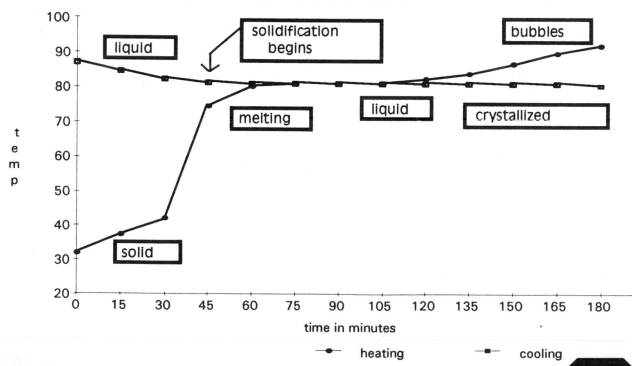

COOLING AND HEATING OF ACETAMIDE

liquid

solidification begins

bubbles

melting

liquid

crystallized

solid

temp

time in minutes

heating   cooling

end of project

Project 39 BIOLOGY REPORT

In this project, you will make all of the set-up decisions. Suggestions for general layout are given below for the two-page report. However, you may design your own layout if you wish. The raw data is given on the following pages.

Add the following: One clip art image of your choice, at least one use of word art or special word effects, and border art if desired. Use color if desired.

Required: Change page set-up for sideways printing.

page 1 layout suggestions

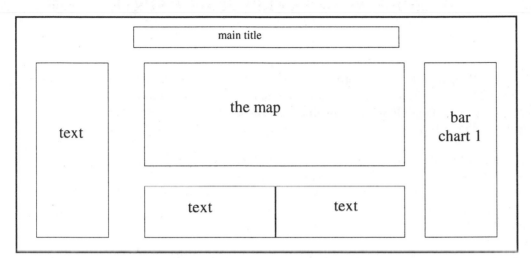

Bar charts:

You may change the style such as to a 3-D style.

Reduce its size, and font sizes in order to fit it in

page 2 layout suggestions

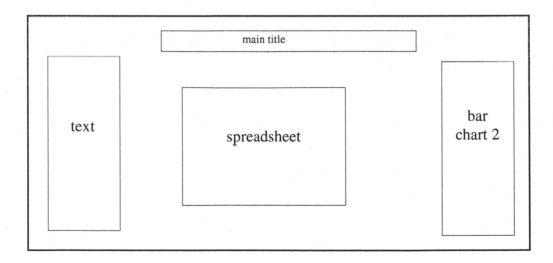

continued on next page

Shown below on this page and the next page is the data that will be included. It will not look this way when placed on your page.

BIOLOGY 304   **BLUEGILL WILDLIFE AREA FISHING SURVEY**   page 1 of 2

BIOLOGY 304   **BLUEGILL WILDLIFE AREA FISHING SURVEY**   page 2 of 2

Description of Area. Bluegill Wildlife Area provides a variety of recreational activities including fishing along 20 miles of Bluegill River. Row boats and sail boats (no motorized craft are permitted) may use Bluegill River and Pintail Lake. Three acres of camping facilities are provided at the end of Bass Road.

Wildlife Refuge. Over 100 acres of unspoiled forest including Oak Lake make up the Wildlife Refuge. This area can be reached by boat only. No hunting or fishing is permitted in this area. It provides critical nesting habitat for birds migrating from South America. Because dead trees are not cut, many woodpeckers such as Common Flickers, Red-bellied Woodpeckers, and Pileated Woodpeckers use the area for nesting.

Fishing. Fishing conditions have improved in recent years due to stocking. Pintail Lake is now rated as the state's top bass fishing areas. Other fish include perch, walleye, catfish, bluegill, and crappie. Perch are becoming scarce, but walleye stocking programs have made them abundant. Annual fishing contests are held on July 4. Last year, two people won $10,000 prizes.

	LAST YEAR			**THIS YEAR**		
FISH	**STOCKED**	**CAUGHT**	**COUNT**	**STOCKED**	**CAUGHT**	**COUNT**
walleye	5000	3890	2890	6000	4440	2280
catfish	2500	2155	1585	3500	2590	1330
bluegill	8400	6211	5677	11760	8702	4469
crappie	7525	4560	2940	10535	7796	4003
other	3300	1890	750	4000	1200	1350

BLUEGILL WILDLIFE AREA FISH SURVEY RESULTS

continued on next page

Shown below on this page is the data that will be included. It will not look this way when placed on your page.

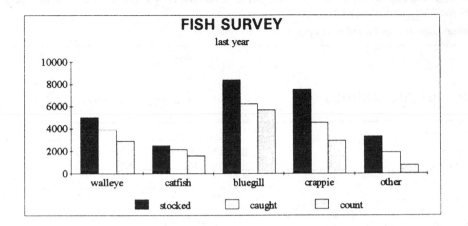

chart 1

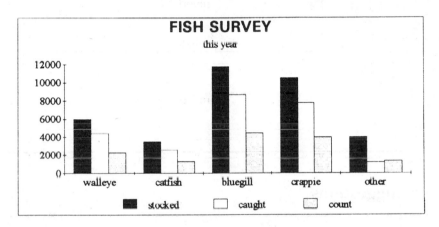

chart 2

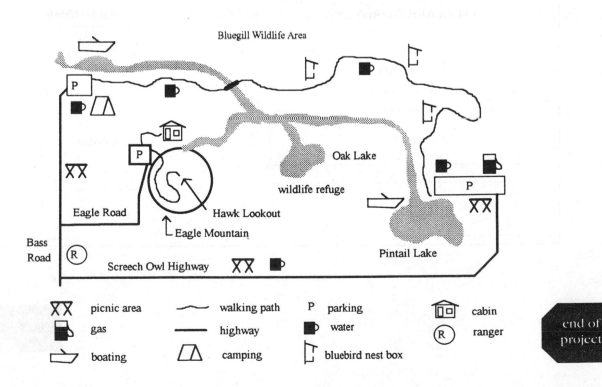

end of project

In this project, you will make all of the set-up decisions. Suggestions for general layout are given below for the two-page report. However, you may design your own layout if you wish. The raw data is given on the following pages.

Add the following: One clip art image of your choice, at least one use of word art or special word effects, and border art if desired. Use color if desired.

Required: Change page set-up for sideways printing.

page 1 layout suggestions

Use titles shown below.

SALES REPORT	YOUR NAME REALTY COMPANY
the house	report 1
paragraph 1	report 2

page 2 layout suggestions

SALES ARE IMPROVING	MODEL HOME
paragraph 2	paragraph 3
chart 1	floor plan 1
chart 2	floor plan 2

continued on next page

Project 40 SALES REPORT (continued)

Shown below on this page and the next page is the data that will be included. It will not look this way when placed on your page.

Directions

Database list screen
1. Use your database software to enter the data shown below.
2. Create two database reports (shown on next page) from the data just entered.

3. If database software is not available, you could place the data and reports in tables.

salesperson	date	city	street	house	style	age	sale price
Antonio	January 02	Parma Hts.	Pecan Lane	501	colonial	6	$50,300
Consuelo	January 05	Fort Worth	Mulberry St.	257	ranch	7	$85,000
Antonio	January 08	Chagrin Falls	Nannyberry	697	cape cod	15	$120,500
Consuelo	January 11	Miami Beach	Hemlock Rd.	438	ranch	22	$92,100
Antonio	January 14	Fort Worth	Chinaberry St.	772	log	8	$150,600
Consuelo	January 17	Miami Beach	Locast Ave.	661	colonial	6	$145,800
Antonio	January 20	Parma Hts.	Silverbell Lane	338	tudor	17	$165,000
Consuelo	January 23	Fort Worth	Dogwood Trail	1467	colonial	20	$98,000
Antonio	January 26	Chagrin Falls	Willow St.	2288	ranch	8	$72,900
Consuelo	January 29	Miami Beach	Palm Ave.	9911	cape cod	6	$124,500
Antonio	February 01	Fort Worth	Sassafras St.	1321	ranch	14	$95,000
Consuelo	February 04	Miami Beach	Oak Rd.	590	log	8	$62,200
Antonio	February 07	Chagrin Falls	Hawthorn St.	666	colonial	5	$69,500
Consuelo	February 10	Chagrin Falls	Possumhaw Rd.	646	tudor	17	$79,800

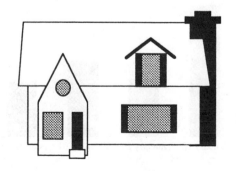

continued on next page

Shown below on this page and the next page is the data that will be included. It will not look this way when placed on your page.

Report 1   Sales for Antonio

date	salesperson	city	street	house	style	age
January 02	Antonio	Parma Hts.	Pecan Lane	501	colonial	6
January 08	Antonio	Chagrin Falls	Nannyberry Ave.	697	cape cod	15
January 14	Antonio	Fort Worth	Chinaberry St.	772	log	8
January 20	Antonio	Parma Hts.	Silverbell Lane	338	tudor	17
January 26	Antonio	Chagrin Falls	Willow St.	2288	ranch	8
February 01	Antonio	Fort Worth	Sassafras St.	1321	ranch	14
February 07	Antonio	Chagrin Falls	Hawthorn St.	666	colonial	5

COUNT:
7

sort   query

Report 2   Sales for Consuelo

date	salesperson	city	street	house	style	age
January 05	Consuelo	Fort Worth	Mulberry St.	257	ranch	7
January 11	Consuelo	Miami Beach	Hemlock Rd.	438	ranch	22
January 17	Consuelo	Miami Beach	Locast Ave.	661	colonial	6
January 23	Consuelo	Fort Worth	Dogwood Trail	1467	colonial	20
January 29	Consuelo	Miami Beach	Palm Ave.	9911	cape cod	6
February 04	Consuelo	Miami Beach	Oak Rd.	590	log	8
February 10	Consuelo	Chagrin Falls	Possumhaw Rd.	646	tudor	17

COUNT:
7

sort   query

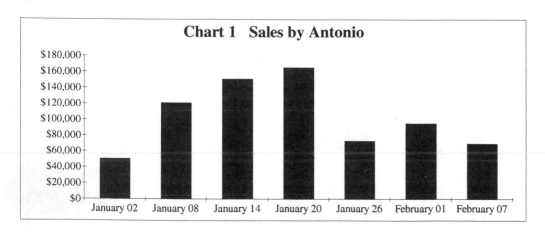

Chart 1   Sales by Antonio

continued on next page

74

Shown below is the data that will be included. It will not look this way when placed on your page.

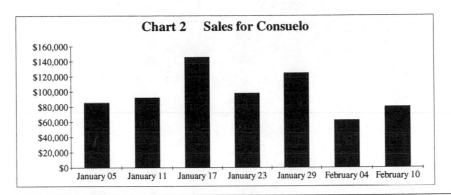

Chart 2   Sales for Consuelo

paragraph 1

Sales have continued to improve over the last two months despite a minor slump in the market in February. We forecast that the sales will pick up near the end of February and continue to improve as the weather warms up. The February slump seems to have occurred just as the Federal Reserve increased interest rates. Interest rates should stabilize within three weeks.

paragraph 2

As the charts below show, our two salespersons are doing an excellent job. I will recommend to our central office that both receive a bonus this year. Our new computerized listing service has been a big factor in their success. When a buyer comes to our office, we can show them pictures of the house on the computer. It can also display room layouts, and a map of the neighborhood.

paragraph 3

We are proud to announce our new model home as shown below. The floor plan reflects changes demanded by first time buyers. The key selling point is a huge living room with fireplace. Direct access to the living room from the front porch adds a sense of openness not seen in previous plans. Another change is a wall between the living room and dining room. This adds a sense of coziness to the living room but allows for openness when desired by opening the folding door.

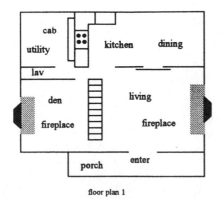

floor plan 1

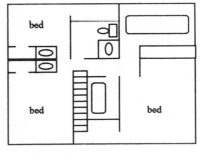

floor plan 2

end of project

75

APPENDIX
Basic Design Principles for Desktop Publishing

Basic Design Principles

by L. Joyce Arnston and Carol Nordquist[1]

Let's look at some general design principles as you begin to plan publications. You may find that the planning process will be the most important step as you put together the elements for the total picture.

First, the purpose of design is to help convey the message. If you are not careful, the design elements can overpower the message you wish to communicate. A good design should complement as well as improve the communication of the message.

The purpose of design is to help convey the message.

Second, there are no design principles that are set in concrete. In other words, these principles are fluid and are to be applied as appropriate to publications. As you probably have guessed, this is a highly subjective topic. One cannot necessarily apply the same principles among various publications, and what applies to one may not apply at all to another. All desktop publishers should be willing to experiment with a publication to explore effective means of imparting the desired message. How the message is delivered will, of course, vary with the audience and content.

Desktop publishers should be willing to experiment.

There are, however, some good rules of thumb for publication design. Let's take a look at some important considerations.

The Purpose of the Publication

The first rule of publication design is this: **Make sure you know the purpose of the publication.** Determine its goals and message. Are you trying to be informative? Sell something? Motivate the reader? What are the key points that should be emphasized?

Make sure you know the purpose of the publication.

Appropriateness to the Audience

The second rule of publication design emphasizes the importance of speaking to the reader in the proper way to convey the message. **Make sure you know the audience.** Many a message has been lost because it was not created with the correct audience in mind.

Make sure you know the audience.

---

[1] Reprinted from *Concepts and Applications for the Desktop Publisher: An Introduction* (Cincinnati: South-Western Publishing, 1994). Reprinted by permission of South-Western Publishing Company.

You must try to customize the publication to fit the reader. Consider such factors as age and educational level. Will this reader, like most, prefer shorter words and sentences? What will get the reader to take time to read the publication?

It is also important to apply design elements appropriately to make the publication interesting and inviting. Remember not to get too complex; simplicity is often the best policy in both layout and vocabulary.

Feedback can be given by readers, depending on the purpose of the publication. Include a response card or a telephone number for them to use to write or call with questions or orders. Note in the illustration below the registration form that is included in the brochure.

Consistency

A publication should be consistent in fonts, colors, margins, and design elements.

Consistency is another fundamental issue to consider. A publication should be consistent from page to page in fonts, color, margins, and design elements. The brochure below illustrates these concerns.

Organization

Organization is as valuable in the production of a publication as it is in the writing.

Organization is as valuable in the production of a publication as it is in the writing. A well-organized design supports continuity. It groups related items and highlights what is important. A poorly organized design impedes reading and detracts from even the best-written messages.

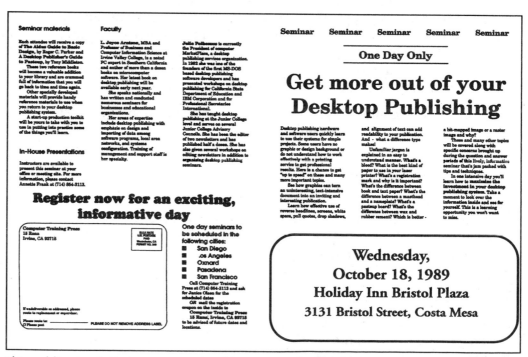

This publication is appropriate to its audience, uses feedback, is consistent in typography, is organized, and has an effective mix of graphic elements.

The Graphic Element Mix

It is important that the design be a good balance of text and graphics. Be careful that your layout—vertically, horizontally, or diagonally—isn't too text-intensive. A text-intensive page can be boring. Use graphics to break up the text into small bites. But be aware that too many graphic elements can detract from the message.

Sometimes it is difficult to locate a graphic that will serve the purpose of the publication. In that case, look for ways to use color, white space, borders, or special text effects such as bulleted lists. Always try to balance the publication design. Notice the application of these principles in the illustration of the brochure.

Your designs should contain a good balance of text and graphics.

Making Decisions on Type

The type you choose for your publication is one of the basic elements in the overall design. The typeset word is important for both what and how something is said; the typography must contribute to the message, not detract from it.

It is important to choose a typeface that matches the message of your publication. Type can help to deliver your message, harm the delivery, or not affect it. Type can set a formal or an informal mood and can make a publication easier to read. Some typefaces work better with certain publication formats and content, and they allow you to get your point across more easily.

Desktop publishing gives you many options in terms of selecting and arranging type to get a specific message across to the reader. Choose a typeface that is attractive, readable, and compatible with your publication. It is a good idea to select one type family such as Helvetica or Palatino for headlines and another such as Times Roman for body copy. Boldface, italic, and shadow variations within the typeface family can then be used for captions and type-based graphic effects.

Choose a typeface that is attractive, readable, and compatible with your publication.

Avoid using too many typefaces or type styles in a single publication. You should not use more than two or three. Remember that consistency is important. The same typefaces should be used for the same elements throughout the document. Use different sizes of type to bring out the separate levels within the publication.

Body Text   Serif typefaces are used for most body text because they are quite readable even at small sizes. Italic, script, and ornamental typefaces are difficult to read. If you want to convey an informal mood, consider setting your body text flush left; to connote formality and orderliness, use justified type.

Avoid using too many typefaces or type styles in a publication.

The Nonesuch Players
present
Murder after Hours
starring

RODNEY CASTILE *as* Major Sidwell
MARGARET TUPPENCE *as* Ms. Dane
EMMA CASTILE *as* General Sidwell
WILBUR TUPPENCE *as* Mr. Dane
SPARKY *as* Fido

"Not as bad as you'd expect..."
Ralph Rodney
The Times

A brand-new mystery from the pen of H.H. Bardoff.

Never seen before!

In the comfort of our newly refurbished theater

August 25-September 4!

TICKETS SELLING FAST!   555-6731

Text should range between 9 and 12 points.

Another important question is what size of type to use. Readers do not like small type; the size of your type may determine whether or not your publication will be read. Text should range between 9 and 12 points for best readability.

A good rule of thumb is to use at least one point more of leading than the type size.

Leading plays an important role in readability. Too much or too little vertical space makes text hard to read. A good rule of thumb is to use at least one point more of leading than the type size. For example, if you are using 10-point type, use at least 11 points of leading. It is important that the lines of body text not look cramped or "lost" in the white space.

FACTORS THAT AFFECT READABILITY

Typeface	**Choose a serif typeface for body text.**
Type size	**Body text should be from 9 to 12 points.**
Type style	**Normal is best for body text.**
Line length	**Apply the ease of reading rule.**
Paper	**What will the text look like when printed?**
Leading	**Use at least a point more than the type size.**
Kerning	**Kern headlines manually.**
Hyphenation	**Both excessive hyphenation and too much space between words should be avoided.**

A readable publication has line breaks often enough to prevent monotony without causing the reader to jump from line to line.

which is the object of headlines. They contrast well with the serif typefaces generally used for body text and provide a visual break from long blocks of serif copy.

Headlines A simple sans serif typeface is often more legible in headlines. As you have learned, sans serif typefaces attract attention,

Headlines should be larger than body text—14 points or more—and proportional to the column width and the size of the article.

When you use headlines in a document, you want them to stand out as headlines but not distract from the text that follows. Headlines should be larger than body text—14 points or more—and proportional to the column width and the size of the article. They are often bold and left aligned, but you can center them if your text is justified. Unless a headline is very short, uppercase and lowercase should be used rather than all capital letters for ease in reading.

If a headline is more than one line, you need to be careful in breaking it (for example, do not break a word at the end of a line). Split a headline where it makes sense.

YOUR SELF-CONFIDENCE GOOD HORSE SENSE TODAY

What does a racehorse have that you don't? Or, to put it another way, why will people gamble their money freely, sometimes blindly, on a horse, when they are afraid to place the same degree of confidence in a bet on themselves?

Your Best Bet

What does a racehorse have that you don't? Or, to put it another way, why will people gamble their money freely, sometimes blindly, on a horse, when they are afraid to place the same degree of confidence in a bet on themselves?

Like other elements, headlines should be treated consistently throughout a document. For example, if you use an initial cap and left alignment for the first headline, make sure all equivalent headlines are keyed the same way.

An ineffective and an effective headline

Paper and Page Size

Pages commonly are 8.5 by 11 inches. Although other sizes may be used, this choice is usually the most economical. Page size is determined by the type of publication you are creating.

Page Orientation

Page orientation is an important layout decision. Portrait and landscape are the options. **Portrait** is a tall, vertical orientation; **landscape** is wide or horizontal (see illustration). Orientation should be determined by the type of information you will be presenting in the publication.

Landscape and portrait orientation

Portrait orientation, the most common format, is more comfortable to read. It uses fewer and more narrow columns. Portrait orientation is used for reports and most newsletters.

Landscape orientation allows more columns that can be wider. It generally is used for documents that are composed of tables, charts, or graphs. This orientation is good for tri-fold brochures.

Do not mix the two orientations. Make reading the publication easy for your audience.

Choosing a Focal Point

For DTP publications, you will be using a combination of text and graphics. It will be important to position each of the elements precisely in a visually pleasing way to communicate the message. To be visually pleasing, you need to consider how people read.

Whether you are laying out a one-page publication or a publication with facing pages, there is a natural optical center, the point where the eye glances first. The optical center is a point above the mathematical center about two-thirds of the page up from the bottom. The accompanying figure compares the optical and the geographic center of a page.

We know, in general, that the eye views from left to right and from top to bottom.

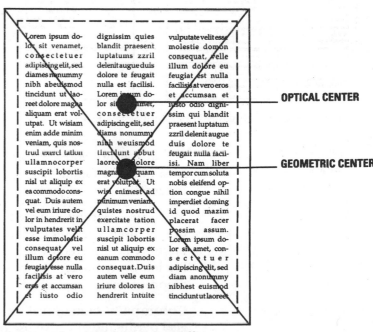

OPTICAL CENTER

GEOMETRIC CENTER

The optical center of a page is different from its geographic center.

The document should be designed to keep this flow in mind. Readers glance first at headlines; then they look at photographs, captions, and other graphic elements; and then they read the text.

The desktop publisher creates a **focal point,** the center of interest on a page or set of facing pages. The center of interest draws the reader's eye to a headline, graphic, or other design element. Then the desktop publisher lays out the path he or she wants the reader to follow.

Take great care in choosing a focal point. If you design a page so the eye is drawn to the bottom right corner, the normal path for a reader is to move to the next page. You have encouraged the reader to skip the page. If you draw attention to the bottom of the page, the article or image should be interesting enough to make the reader move to the top of the page and read everything.

White Space

The use of white or nonprinted space is important for effective design. The white space created by margins, columns, and line lengths must set off the text without detracting from its readability, and it must make the text and graphic presentation attractive. White space is sometimes thought of as a graphic element because it can focus attention on important text and graphics.

If you have narrow margins, the text will appear to be squeezed on the page with no breathing room. On the other hand, you must be careful not to have too much white space, making the text look lost on the page as in the accompanying illustration.

If a document is set up in long blocks of text, separate paragraphs with space and indent the start of each paragraph. This arrangement gives the reader the page organization at a glance. Most WP and DTP programs come with tabs defaulting to at least every half-inch, making it easy to indent a paragraph the standard indentation.

Too little or too much white space makes text hard to read.

Margins   Margins can create a feeling of space and should affect the size of type used. They set off the text and graphics and provide a framework. Margins are affected by the space available on the page, whether the page is a left or right page, the type of publication, the amount of text and the graphics on the page, the binding, and the width and height of columns.

Columns   Columns make a page easier to read and add interest to it. They also permit the effective use of white space as a graphic. There is no real limit to the number of columns you can use, but generally you will see from one to six. The type of publication you are creating will help you decide how many columns you should have. Other factors to consider include type size, white space, size of graphics, and placement of headings. Column width and number can change from page to page.

A document with a single text column per page is the simplest pattern. This format is often used for business and educational reports, proposals, and other simple internal documents. Many complex one-column publications contain straight running text separated only by subheads.

Single-column layouts are good for smaller page sizes and easily readable typefaces with generous leading. They allow you to present a great deal of unbroken text. Continuous text that will keep the reader interested from line to line works well in this format. A one-column setup is also economical; however, it can be difficult to read and monotonous.

There are several techniques that can be used to enliven single-column publications. The inside margins can be wider to give an open look to the document. A wide left margin can accommodate a special graphic design; a wide right margin, appropriately labeled, can provide a place for notes. Bullets and rules can be used to set off the text.

A two-column format has a more designed and polished look. It is used in many brochures, reports, and catalogs. Two-column pages offer more flexibility and opportunity for creativity, especially if the columns are unequal in width. There may be occasions when you will have to choose a two-column format because of the size of the graphics being used.

The three-column format is the most commonly used in DTP. This format provides more flexibility; three-column documents are also the most readable because the column width is comfortable for the eye to scan. Since the

- **The most common margin is one inch.**
- **For publications containing facing pages, inside margins are often smaller than outside margins. When you open the publication, the inside margins of the two facing pages combine to create the illusion of one margin.**
- **Documents that are double-sided and bound generally have uneven left and right margins that allow for the binding width on the inside. The inside and outside margins do not have to be symmetrical; in fact, uneven margins create interest in applicable publications.**
- **Top margins are like outside margins (one-half to one inch).**
- **Bottom margins are the largest.**

The three column format is the most commonly used in DTP.

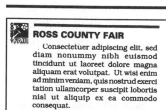

ROSS COUNTY FAIR

Consectetuer adipiscing elit, sed diam nonummy nibh euismod tincidunt ut laoreet dolore magna aliquam erat volutpat. Ut wisi enim ad minim veniam, quis nostrud exerci tation ullamcorper suscipit lobortis nisl ut aliquip ex ea commodo consequat.

Duis autem vel eum iriure dolor in hendrerit in vulputate velit esse molestie consequat.

- Vel illum dolore.
- Feugiat nulla facilisis at vero eros et accumsan.
- Et iusto odio dignissim qui blandit.

Praesent luptatum suscipit lobortis nisl ut aliquip ex ea zzril delenit augue duis dolore te feugait nulla.

The one-column format

GOOD EARTH GIFT BASKET
Show them you care about the Earth as well as them with our attractive basket of organically grown foods from around the country.
65-690 $25.00

REUSABLE GROCERY BAG
Our grocery bags are made of durable 100% cotton, manufactured in the United States.
32-418 $5.00, 6 for $25.00

WHAT A BRIGHT IDEA!
Our high-efficiency light bulbs last 70% longer and cost 35% less to run than conventional bulbs. Specify 60- or 120-watt size.
18-043 $4.95, 6 for $22.00

33

The two-column format

COMPUTERIZE YOUR BUSINESS!

Lorem veripsum dolor sit amet, consectetuer adipiscing elit, sed diames nonummy nibh euismod tincidunt ut laoreet dolorest em magna aliquam verit erat volutpat. Abut wisi enim ad minim veniam, quis nos-trud exercitation

ullamcorper suscipit lobortis nisl ut aliquip ex ea commodost consequat.

Duis autem vel eum iriure dolor in hendrerit in vulpu-tate verit velit esse moles-tie consequat, vel

illum dolore eu feugiat verit nulla facilisis at vero eros et accumsan et iusto odio dignissim qui blanditest praesent luptatum ave zzril delenit augue duis dolore te feugait nulla

The three-column format

Rules can be used to separate columns.

columns are narrower, you may need to choose a smaller type size and left alignment for better readability. This format is good if the publication will contain several illustrations.

The space between columns is called the **gutter** or **alley** and is used to separate the text. Column width often determines the size of the alley. The larger amounts of space between words in justified text may make it necessary to differentiate between columns with a larger alley than will be needed with flush left text.

Rules (horizontal or vertical lines) are sometimes used to separate columns. If you use a rule between columns, ensure that the alley is wide enough so that there is a sufficient amount of white space on both sides of the rule. Since the right margin varies with flush left alignment, column rules may help differentiate between columns. Column rules are largely unnecessary with justified text because the flush right margin clearly defines the columns.

Creating Your Own Publication

Creating a Grid

Webster defines a GRID *as a network of uniformly spaced horizontal and perpendicular lines.*

Webster defines a **grid** as a network of uniformly spaced horizontal and perpendicular lines. Grids were used by Renaissance artists as a method of resizing their sketches to fit the proportions of murals. Architects use grids to scale their drawings. Traditionally, graphic artists use a **blueline grid**—a sheet of paper with nonprinting blue lines made with a special pen—to help design a page. From the time of Gutenberg, typographers have used grids to design and make up printed pages.

The electronic grid used in DTP is a nonprinting overlay or underlying structure of dots or horizontal and vertical lines on the screen that serve as guides but do not print. Most programs allow you to move these guides anywhere on the page. A grid can also include margins and columns. Desktop publishers usually set the grid on the master pages.

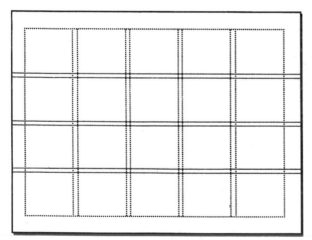

A grid can help you plan your publication.

Grids help desktop publishers place text and images precisely on the page. With some software, the grid lines act like a magnet; this **snap feature** pulls text or graphics that you are placing to the nearest lines on the grid. Some programs come with templates for grids.

Using a grid is a way of looking at the page layout with the specific size, shape, and proportion allowed for text and graphic images. Grids help you maintain consistency, determine an orderly placement of text and graphics, and establish balance on a page.

Importing Text and Graphics

As you assemble text and graphics into your publication, you will appreciate an emphasis on planning. If you have made and executed your design decisions carefully, page composition should proceed easily and smoothly.

As you lay out your text, beware of leaving **widows** (the first line of a paragraph at the bottom of a column or page) and **orphans** (the last line of a paragraph at the top of a column or page). Both seriously interrupt the flow of text. (Note: Various programs define widows and orphans differently.) Watch also for isolated subheads.

Beware of leaving WIDOWS and ORPHANS.

Revising and Refining

Once you have laid out your publication on the desktop, you should print a sample copy. Proofread it carefully, paying particular attention to names and dates. Take time to make any adjustments that will improve the readability of your publication.

Print a sample copy and proofread it carefully.

If your copy is justified, watch for excessive hyphenation. It is important to use hyphens, however, to eliminate **rivers of white**—large spaces between words that give a nonprofessional appearance to the document. Text that is flush left does not require hyphenation unless the ending of a line is extremely shortened because of a long word wrapping at the end of a line.

Use hyphenation to eliminate RIVERS OF WHITE.

Kerning (adjusting the space between pairs of letters) is especially important if you want to make a headline look better. Kerning brings characters closer together or farther apart for readability as well as appearance as in the illustration here. If your DTP software has automatic kerning, there will be very little need to do any manual kerning of body text. Headlines, however, often require some refinement because of their role as attention-getters and because they are often set in larger type—unattractive spacing between letters is more noticeable.

ELLEN GILCHRIST
ELLEN GILCHRIST

Note the difference between unkerned and kerned text.

Printing the Final Copy

After you have corrected your proof copy, all that remains is to print the final. You can print your own master copy on a laser printer, or you may decide to take your publication on disk to a commercial printer so that it can be output on a typesetter.

NOTES

NOTES

NOTES

NOTES